Not content to rest on his laurels as our region's—if not the nation's—foremost writer on the capture and delectation of hard clams, Curtis Badger has produced a culinary moonshot in *A Culinary History of Delmarva*. The foods therein, from black drum to scrapple, marsh hen to crab cakes, are his framework on which to hang a lovely exploration of the Delmarva Peninsula's lands and waters, its history and its human characters. Socrates made much of "an unexamined life" being a life not worth living. The same goes for the places in which we live and have thoughtlessly dominated the rest of nature in recent centuries—unexamined they are doomed to be altered without our even knowing what we're losing. Mr. Badger's book is as fine a start as any toward an examination of what made the Delmarva Peninsula unique and delightsome, toward making it a place truly worth living in.

—Tom Horton
Chesapeake Bay author, advocate and educator

A CULINARY HISTORY OF DELMARVA

From the Bay to the Sea

CURTIS J. BADGER

Published by American Palate
A Division of The History Press
Charleston, SC
www.historypress.com

All images are from the author's collection unless otherwise noted.
Front cover, bottom: strawberry auction, 1926, photo by Jeff Vaughan.

First published 2021

ISBN 9781540247049

Library of Congress Control Number: 2020951875

CONTENTS

FOREWORD

In *A Culinary History of Delmarva: From the Bay to the Sea*, Curtis J. Badger shows how the region's landscape, wildlife, agricultural produce and history combined to create a distinctive local cuisine. Badger is well qualified for the task. An outdoorsman, he knows intimately the peninsula's seductive entanglement of soil and salt water. He has dipped for crabs, fished for spot and swelling toads, gathered clams and oysters and hunted for ducks and marsh hens. A naturalist, he has studied the habits of clams, muskrats and diamondback terrapins and photographed birds and wildfowl innumerable. A historian, he understands how the expansion in the late nineteenth century of the regional transportation network led to the near destruction of local terrapin and shorebird populations and how the rise early in the following century of the Eastern Shore of Virginia Produce Exchange created an empire built on Irish potatoes. As a cook, he is thoroughly acquainted with traditional ways of preparing local fare.

Badger recognizes the transcendent quality of Delmarva foodways. For the people of the peninsula, the dishes that they prepare are more than good things to eat. They are representative of three hundred years of tilling this earth, of fishing these creeks and bays, of gunning these marshes and of tending fires and cooking meals. They are a tangible connection with elders and ancestors. They are a cultural tradition that one can actually taste.

—Brooks Miles Barnes
Onancock, Virginia
May 18, 2020

ACKNOWLEDGEMENTS

The title of this book is *A Culinary History of Delmarva*. To begin with, in the interest of full disclosure, I am not a historian. Way back in college days, I recall taking one history class, which was rather ambitiously called "The History of Western Civilization." To be honest, I found Western Civilization boring.

I like to tell stories, and I like food, and that is how this book came to be. When I was in school, history was a blur of names and dates and battles, all to be committed to memory. I've never thought of history in this fashion. To me, history is an infinite succession of stories. Some stories overlap, and some neatly begin and end. History is a living narrative, an unending supply chain of stories.

The stories in this book come from many sources, but one in particular needs to be cited. That would be a website called "The Countryside Transformed: The Railroad and the Eastern Shore of Virginia, 1870–1935." The site was created in 2008 by Brooks Miles Barnes of the Eastern Shore Public Library and William G. Thomas III of the University of Virginia's Virginia Center for Digital History. It is now supported by the university's Institute for Advanced Technology in the Humanities and can be accessed at eshore.iath.virginia.edu. It is an archive of newspapers, maps, photographs, manuscripts, public documents and other media, and while the stated goal was to document how the coming of the railroad in 1884 changed the mental and physical landscape of the Virginia Eastern Shore, it does far more than that. To paraphrase Forrest Gump, it's like opening a box of chocolates.

Many of us are interested in history, but few have the discipline or the inclination to spend hours going through court documents, wills, deeds and census records. "The Countryside Transformed" brings history to life and makes it accessible. You can read the October 10, 1882 issue of the *Peninsula Enterprise* newspaper and experience in real time how the community was reacting as the NYP&N Railroad made its way south. You can also read personal accounts of visits to barrier island gunning clubs, and you can read about farm news, society news, crime news and all the important headlines of the day.

Coinciding with the publication of this book, a new regional library will be opening in the town of Parksley, Virginia—an old railroad town, by the way—and in a wing of the library will be the Eastern Shore Heritage Center, a new resource that brings to life what "Countryside Transformed" accomplished digitally. Fittingly, the space housing the new collection will be named for Dr. Barnes.

The new Eastern Shore Heritage Center will join a long list of resources available to those who are interested in the history of the Delmarva Peninsula. The list would include the Eastern Shore Barrier Islands Center in Machipongo, Virginia; the Nabb Center and the Ward Museum at Salisbury University; the Chesapeake Bay Maritime Museum in St. Michaels; and the Lewes Public Library and the Lewes Museum in Delaware.

A book about food would not be complete without acknowledging those who provide it. Many of us have our home gardens, but for those who do not, dozens of communities on Delmarva have farmers' markets, providing not only fresh local fruits and vegetables but also meats, seafood, baked goods and jellies and preserves.

Hog killing is a thing of the past, but local companies provide meats very much like those our grandparents enjoyed. I strongly suspect that Kirby and Holloway's sage sausage is made with my grandmother's recipe.

Hughes Delaware Maid scrapple is likewise reminiscent of the days when scrapple was made in the kitchen of the farmhouse. The only problem is, it's only available in Delaware. That means every time we visit Lewes, we stop at Lloyd's Market, head to the cooler in the right rear corner of the store and stock up. We've learned how to freeze scrapple. You slice it, put sheets of parchment paper between the slices and then put the slices in a freezer bag and freeze it. The paper prevents the slices from sticking together, so when you want some scrapple, you just take out however many slices you want and heat them up in a nonstick skillet. You don't even have to thaw them.

Lloyd's of Lewes is one of many retailers on Delmarva that deal with local suppliers. Most of Lloyd's meats and produce are sourced locally, and there are similar small businesses throughout the peninsula. In Virginia, where we live, Matthews Market in Mappsville has a reputation for its fresh meats, cut to order in the store. Quail Cove in Machipongo grows and sells organic sweet potatoes and other local produce and meats. Northampton County farmer William Baines is carrying on the Delmarva tradition of producing extraordinary strawberries. When we want seafood, we visit Edwards Seafood or Eastern Shore Seafood in Onley. Both buy from local watermen and employ local folks to cook, pick and pack their crab meat. It doesn't get any fresher. Susan's Seafood in New Church deals with local watermen, and the offerings in her display case change on a daily basis, depending on what the watermen are catching. In winter, she offers fresh muskrats taken by a local trapper.

Over the past few generations, we have experienced a widening gap in the way we grow, gather and consume our food. We no longer have hog killings, and few of us have ever butchered an animal, plucked a chicken or ground our own wheat to make flour. The separation between creating food and consuming food has created a vacuum that increasingly makes us oblivious to the source of what we eat. I hope this book might help eliminate this void, at least to the extent that when we enjoy a good meal, we do so with thoughtfulness and appreciation for where it came from.

INTRODUCTION

In 2012, while working on the book *Exploring Delmarva*, it occurred to me that the people who live in the three states that make up our peninsula have a great deal in common. Remove the geopolitical boundaries—the state lines—and you find communities with a very close kinship and people who have many similarities in their history and culture. We live in a mostly rural environment. Our lives are closely tied to the land and certainly to the water that surrounds us. We hunt and fish, we farm and raise corn and tomatoes in our gardens. We go clamming and crabbing. We enjoy being on the water and hate to contemplate life away from it.

We even gather and prepare our food in a similar manner. For example, you could go anywhere on Delmarva—from Rock Hall to Cape Charles—and ask someone the best way to cook spot, and you'd get the same answer. Spot should be fried, never broiled or baked, and certainly never poached. Purists will tell you the head and tail should be left on. Purists of a certain age will tell you the head and tail should be left on and the spot should be fried in bacon drippings.

If you cross the Chesapeake Bay and head one hundred miles inland, you'll have trouble finding anyone who knows what a spot is, much less how to cook one.

The history and culture of Delmarva are reflected in our food more than in any other medium. Travel up and down the peninsula and you'll find similarities in how we gather food, how we prepare it and the rituals we go through in sharing and consuming it.

A Culinary History of Delmarva examines in depth the foodways of Delmarva—that is, the methods of gathering, preparing and consuming food that are part of our peninsula. Not surprisingly, many of these foodways are derived from our natural environment, the forests, bays, creeks and marshes that have fed us well for many centuries.

This book contains recipes for classic Delmarva dishes, but it is not a recipe book in the conventional sense. Instead, it examines the rituals of gathering, preparing and consuming foods that are indigenous to Delmarva, and it considers how these are related to our environment and history.

Invaluable windows into Delmarva's foodways of the past are old recipe books, and I search used bookstores and antique markets for them as often as I can. One such example is *Housekeeper's Companion*, compiled by Bessie E. Gunter of Accomac, Virginia, which was published in 1889 and is a pioneer among cookbooks published to raise funds for worthy causes. Profits from *Housekeeper's Companion* aided the building fund of Drummondtown Baptist Church.

In her preface to the book, Ms. Gunter points out that many of the "receipts" had been used by contributors' families for several generations, meaning that many predate the Civil War. Eighty-nine men and women contributed favorite recipes to the collection, which, given the proximity of Accomac to the water, is understandably strong in the area of seafood. There are dozens of recipes for fish, oysters, clams, terrapin and lobster, but the compiler did not neglect the sweet tooth. A large section of the book is devoted to cakes, cookies, candies and puddings. Even in those days, one did not subsist on shellfish alone.

A wonderful collection of Maryland recipes is included in *Maryland's Way*, a collection of traditional recipes representing three centuries of Maryland cooking. The book was published as a fundraiser in 1963 by the Hammond–Harwood House Association, which maintains this 1774 Colonial landmark in Annapolis. The book includes photographs by the legendary Maryland photographer A. Aubrey Bodine.

One of the best windows into historic Maryland cooking is *Fifty Years in a Maryland Kitchen* by Mrs. B.C. Howard. Mrs. Howard was born Jane Grant Gilmor in 1801 and at the age of sixteen married Benjamin Chew Howard. Together, they raised twelve children, and along the way Mrs. Howard found time to put together a collection of her recipes for her children, cousins and other kin.

Many of the recipes are believed to have come from "The Vinyard," the Gilmor family estate in Baltimore County, which, judging from the richness of her recipes, must have been a land of abundance. But Mrs. Howard also credits many of the recipes to old English and French cookbooks. She was well known in her day for her skills as a hostess and her lavish and extravagant meals. *Harper's Magazine* was so impressed with her cookery that it published an article on her in an 1882 issue.

Mrs. Howard died at the age of eighty-nine in 1890, leaving behind a treasure of recipes that demonstrate how those with abundant larders lived in the mid-nineteenth century. Her book, first published in 1873, was revised by Florence Brobeck and republished by M. Barrows and company of New York in 1944. A Dover edition was published in 1986. Original copies show up now and then in antiquarian bookstores. Although Mrs. Howard did not have the good fortune to have lived on Delmarva, she certainly knew what to do with terrapins, clams and other foods we call our own.

Local cookbooks, many published by churches as fundraisers, provide witness to the types of food people enjoyed and how they prepared it. Many are unpretentious publications, but most have a special character. *The Parish House Cook Book*, for example, was published by the Women of Hungars Church in Northampton County, Virginia, in 1959. The 115 recipes are written in longhand, each in the script of its author, and it gives the book an heirloom quality, as if each recipe just came from the kitchen of the cook, perhaps a sheen of butter on a lower corner.

For years, we have used a seafood dressing made from a recipe in a cookbook published by a local Baptist church. It is a very simple recipe and it includes ketchup, which likely heightens the pomposity level of food snobs. You mix a tablespoon of ketchup with a tablespoon of horseradish, two tablespoons of mayonnaise and one stalk of celery, finely chopped. It makes a wonderful crab salad. We call it Baptist church dressing.

Delmarva foodways did not evolve from thin air. Some traditions of gathering and cooking food were brought from Europe by early settlers, and many show a later European influence, such as Mrs. Howard's crediting old French and English cookbooks for some of her recipes. Africans brought with them many traditions associated with planting, harvesting and preparing food. Early settlers no doubt learned survival skills from Native Americans, especially in harvesting and cooking local seafood and wild game, which were abundant in our waterways and forests.

Jane Howard, author of *Fifty Years in a Maryland Kitchen*, had a contemporary in a Scottish kitchen during roughly those same fifty years, and the publication of the cookbooks bear remarkable similarities. Mrs. Howard's collection of recipes was reissued years after her death as a tribute and testimony to her skills in the kitchen.

In 1909, a book was published in the United Kingdom called *The Cookery Book of Lady Clark of Tillypronie*, edited by Catherine Frere. It is a collection of recipes collected by Lady Clark, who lived at the sporting estate called Tillypronie in the Scottish Highlands. Lady Clark collected the recipes between 1841 and 1897, and it was published after her death at the request of her husband, Lord John F. Clark, who worked in the British diplomatic service. It was published as a tribute and testimony to her skills in the kitchen.

On Delmarva, we often think of regional dishes as our own creation. Chesapeake Bay crab cakes, for example, originated in the villages and towns that lie near the bay. Right?

Perhaps. But regional cooking did not exist in a vacuum. Lady Clark had a recipe called Crab Kromeskies, which she received from a woman named Ruth Camp in 1882. The recipe calls for flaked cold crab meat held together with a light sauce. The mixture was seasoned with cayenne, formed into balls or patties, coated with a batter and deep fried in lard. It could be a prototype for what we consider original Chesapeake Bay crab cakes.

And so, could our local crab cakes have cousins in the Highlands of Scotland?

SECTION I

On the Water, from Subsistence to Sport

Chapter 1

A GREAT STORE OF FISH

The art of fishing and preparing them for the table is perhaps the most vivid reminder of the uniqueness of Delmarva foodways. The first permanent European settlers were taught how to catch and preserve fish by Native Americans, and we have been at it ever since. Fishing has been a means of survival, a backbone of our economy, our most popular outdoor sport and an avenue of relaxation and recreation. And fish have graced our tables in myriad ways.

On Delmarva, we eat fish that many people have never even heard of. We have them fried and baked, roasted over charcoal, poached, boiled and broiled. In our family, having salted fish with eggs and bacon is a Christmas morning tradition. We eat toads and pigfish, hardheads and spot, sand mullet, spade fish, rock, shark, skate, flounder, white perch, blues, black drum and red drum and black wills. We remove the roe sacs from trout and croakers and fry the roe with scrambled eggs. We leave the head and tail on spot when we fry them because we believe leaving the head on preserves that rich oily-fishy flavor, and as for the tail, it provides a single, wonderful, crispy bite unlike anything that ever came off a store shelf.

Many of us who live on Delmarva prefer fish that seldom show up in the display cases of seafood markets. This is probably a reflection of how our great-grandparents caught and marketed their fish many years ago. If you came from a fishing family, the most valuable fish your grandpop brought in went straight to the market. The flounder, gray trout, rockfish and channel bass were among the quality fish that paid the rent and bought the morning coffee. Grandpop brought home the spot, sand mullet, black wills, white perch, croakers and swelling toads. Grandma would fry these up in a cast-iron skillet shimmering with bacon drippings. And there would be hot cornbread, butterbeans and tomatoes from the garden and tall glasses of sweet tea sweating in the summer heat. This is how we learned to eat fish, and even today I still prefer a plate of fried spot to the more marketable but infinitely more boring flounder. It is an ancient tradition passed down by our British ancestors, who sent the valuable catch to market and brought home the less marketable, but nonetheless tasty, fish to feed the family. According to author Jeffrey Kacirk's *The Word Museum*, the British called these fish *rabble-fish*.

These are the food habits of the coast, traditions that have been passed along for generations until they have become part of our history and culture, unique to our people and our region, a product of the rich landscape of creeks and bays, salt marshes and barrier islands. Go to a restaurant in, let's say, Roanoke and ask for a platter of fried pigfish with the heads and tails left on and see where that gets you. Roanoke is a wonderful city, but Roanoke doesn't know fish.

Eating fish didn't begin as a reflection of our history and culture. Eating fish was a means of survival, and it was something we didn't take to right away. James Wharton wrote a booklet titled *The Bounty of the Chesapeake: Fishing in Colonial Virginia* as part of an educational packet marking the 350th anniversary of the Jamestown settlement in 1957. Wharton depicted early settlers as ineffective fishermen who, despite a wealth of finfish and shellfish in local waters, often died of starvation.

Visits to the New World prior to the Jamestown settlement painted a picture of great bounty. Thomas Heriot accompanied Sir Walter Raleigh when he explored Roanoke Island, North Carolina, in 1585, and he wrote of a wealth of sturgeon, herring and many other fish, as well as crabs, oysters, tortoises, mussels and scallops. The Native people caught fish in weirs made of strong reeds, Heriot wrote, and they speared them from boats or while wading in shallow water.

Captain Samuel Argall, who was specially commissioned by England to fish off the coast to support the Jamestown colony, visited the barrier islands of Delmarva in 1610 and reported "a great store of fish, both shellfish and other."

The reports of the abundance of marine life were probably valid, according to Wharton. But "the infinite plenty was one thing," he wrote. "Making constant and profitable use of it was another."

Early colonists along the bay were not skilled fishermen, the equipment they brought from England was inadequate and they had no means of preserving a good day's catch for use at a later time. And instead of planting garden plots, they raised tobacco, which they believed a more profitable commodity. And so there was starvation in a land of plenty. Luckily, for a while, Native Americans were willing to help them out.

Regarding the early settlers, Wharton said very few had come equipped for fishing. "Their seines were as old fashioned as those used by the Apostles in the New Testament, the simple kind you lowered from a boat and dragged ashore. The Indians had taught them how to spear large fish and erect weirs out of stakes and brushwood to ensnare migrating schools. Such methods worked well enough during the season. But in cold weather, when provisions ran low, scarcely any fish were present in the bay proper."

Within a few years, those setting sail from England to the New World were required to demonstrate usable skills such as fishing, net making, boat building and salt making. On Smith Island, in Northampton County near the tip of Delmarva, salt was made by evaporating sea water, and this important commodity helped preserve fish and other food for the Jamestown colony.

A 1612 account written by William Strachey told of "great shoals of herring and sturgeon" and shad a yard long. Strachey also described what might be the original oyster stew or seafood chowder. The Indians, he said, would boil oysters and mussels together in the same pot and thicken the liquid with "the flour of their wheat." Could it be that we have the Native Americans to thank for the practice of making a roux to thicken soups and stews?

Wharton wrote that Alexander Whitaker in 1613 made the first recorded mention of "torope," or small turtle. The term originated with the Native Americans and referred to the diamondback terrapin, which was unknown in Europe but was to become "an indispensable course on menus designed for the entertainment of royalty and the discriminating elect."

Wharton speculated that the colonists ate their terrapin Indian fashion: "roasted whole in live coals and opened at the table where the savory meat was extracted by appreciative fingers."

The word *terrapin* is said to be a Native American term meaning "edible turtle."

Chapter 2

SALTING FISH

In 1610, the ability to salt fish was a matter of life and death. Today, it is a way of reminding ourselves how our great-great-grandparents lived, a method of preserving and preparing food that links our lives with theirs. We no longer have to preserve fish and other meats with salt, but our family does so, out of habit, I guess. The taste and texture of the fish bring back childhood memories: Sunday breakfast at the kitchen table before dressing for church, Christmas at my grandmother's house with the aroma of the cedar tree filling the room, bacon and biscuits with fig preserves, and cheesy eggs, with a bit of salted fish dotted with butter.

When we salt fish today, we are not just preserving a source of protein for winter breakfasts; we are capturing the last of the summer season, taking it to the very edge of frost, salting it away in an old stone crock until on a cold, gray morning in January we'll take it out, rinse it off and bring it back to life in the old iron skillet.

I suppose I enjoy the tradition of salting fish as much as I enjoy eating them. It's a process that links the generations, one that is unchanged since the time of the colonists. Our old stone crock has been used for so many years for salting fish that the salt has leached through the glazing and into the clay. No matter how many times we wash it, a white filigree of salt will decorate the dark inner walls of the container as soon as it dries.

We go out in late October, while the bays and creeks still have a few spot, croakers and trout. I prepare the fish by scaling and filleting them and then rinse them in fresh water to remove all blood, which could cause the fish to spoil. Then I pack them in salt in the old crock. A layer of salt, a layer of fish. And so on until I run out of fillets. I cover the crock with a tea towel, place a dinner plate on top to hold it in place and let the fish and the salt begin their chemical reaction, a marriage of earth and sea, holding in suspension the last of the summer as we await a new spring.

For salting, fish must proceed quickly from the bay to the crock. Time is of the essence. Fish that have languished for a day or two in a seafood market refrigerator are useless. The process depends on the salt reacting with the moisture in the tissues of the fish to make a brine, and once taken from the sea, fish dehydrate quickly. When salted when they are very fresh, the meat will remain firm and white throughout the winter. If the fish are allowed to dehydrate before salting, you'll have a crock of yellow, leathery fillets more suitable for shoemaking than Sunday breakfast.

For that reason, it pays to catch your own or to purchase them directly from a local waterman who understands the salting process. In fall, we buy a twenty-five-pound bag of salt and clean out the old crock, anticipating a productive fishing trip. That way we're ready. As soon as we return from a good day on the water, we'll clean the fish and salt them away before attending to the other post-trip chores, such as washing the boat and stowing the fishing tackle.

In a few weeks, the fish and the salt will make a brine, and the fish will become firmer and the meat will be opaque. If we anticipate a Sunday breakfast of fish, we'll take a few fillets out on Saturday, let them soak in fresh water overnight and boil them in water in an iron skillet in the morning. A little butter and black pepper are the only seasonings necessary. And here we have a wonderful Delmarva breakfast from the coast: salted fish, scrambled eggs, crisp bacon and biscuits with butter and fig preserves.

In our health-conscious world, salted fish should be considered an occasional treat and not a regular part of one's diet, especially if there are issues of hypertension. My grandparents and great-grandparents ate them regularly to supplement their steady diet of salted hams, shoulders and sidemeat from the smokehouse, as well as eggs, sausage, scrapple, bacon and other high-fat foods. They lived well into their eighties, worked on a small farm and probably did not stop working long enough during the day to allow fat to accumulate. Our lifestyle is different, and salted fish is the occasional treat—the taste of tradition—not the staple it once was for earlier generations.

Not coincidentally, the first barrier island along the Delmarva coast settled by English explorers was chosen because of its potential for salt making and its proximity to fish and wild game. Captain Samuel Argall explored Smith Island and reported to the acting governor of Virginia, Sir Thomas Dale, that this low-lying barrier beach could be used to distill salt from sea water. Argall's famous boast of "a great store of fish" meant little unless this great store could be preserved in brine for a reasonable length of time to sustain the colony. So, a camp was established on Smith Island, sea water was heated and evaporated in great vats and the salty residue was ground and processed and used to preserve fish and other meats.

Years later, on nearby Mockhorn Island, an inner island with little high land, evaporation ponds were built to extract salt from seawater in what might have been America's first solar-powered industry. According to Ralph T. Whitelaw's *Virginia's Eastern Shore*, John Custis, the great-grandfather of Martha Custis Washington, entered into a contract with Peter Reverdly on April 4, 1668, to make salt on the island, which was owned by Custis. Reverdly was apparently an expert at the salt-making process, and a lengthy contract gave him instructions to build 312 clay-lined evaporation ponds for extracting salt from seawater.

Whitelaw doesn't report on the fate of this business venture, but the lengthy contract, the involvement of a salt-making professional and the very scope of the project are evidence of how precious salt was in the early lives of the people who settled along the coast.

I feel somewhat ashamed that I bought my twenty-five pounds of salt for a modest sum at a local food market. Today, we take salt for granted and even avoid it if possible. But these are special times, and the salting of fish is more a religious act, a way of paying homage, than it is a means of fending off winter famine. I drove to the market in my car, I am writing these words on a computer, in a room heated and cooled by a heat pump.

While I make no salt, cut and split very little wood and seldom depend on my legs to take me significant distances, I'm not so sure my life is that much better than that of my great-grandparents. They took for granted a world that we seem desperately trying to hold in our grasp. In their day, it seemed there would forever be a great store of fish swimming in clean waters from Maine to Florida. And today, the scenario has become reversed. We have a great store of salt. But the fish are becoming precious.

Chapter 3

BOTTOM FISHING

Fishing methods that lack sophistication tend to be the most effective. If it's fish you want to eat, why try to attract them with something made of fur, feather, metal or rubber? Fish rarely have such foods high on their culinary lists. If you want to catch fish, give them what they really want, which usually is another fish of a more modest dimension.

I once had a fleeting urge to be a sophisticated fisherman, so I bought a salt-water fly rod. I had fun whipping the rod around and making the line do all sorts of parlor tricks, but I rarely caught fish. So I snipped off the fly, tied on a hook, baited it with squid and began having a fine old time with the croakers.

A friend who lived in the suburbs of Washington, D.C., who was a for-real sophisticated fisherman, one day asked me how I was doing with the fly rod. "Great," I said, "catching all kinds of croakers."

"What are you catching them on?"

"Squid," I said.

"How do you tie it?"

"What do you mean tie it? I cut off a slice and put it on the hook."

He gave me his best Felix Unger look, and the next time he visited, he brought me a box of six beautiful imitation squid strips made from the downy feathers of a snow goose tummy. They look great on my office shelf.

What I do is called bottom fishing, and I suspect that phrase carries implications that go beyond the fact that I locate my bait at or near the bottom of the particular creek I'm fishing. Bottom fisherman. Bottom feeder. It doesn't look good on one's résumé.

Surf fishing on one of the seaside barrier islands.

But it does look good on one's platter, and that's the entire point, isn't it? We're talking about real food here, not sophistication, not athleticism, not guile and cunning and the ability to pluck the tummy of a snow goose and turn that goose down into a deadly weapon that, if presented with just the proper touch, the proper drift, will entice a croaker to inhale it, thus impaling itself, and after a brief but exciting skirmish end up amid cool eelgrass in the bottom of one's custom-made hand-woven creel from Farlow's of London.

Lordy. All I wanted was some fish for dinner.

Unlike the early colonists at Jamestown, we no longer have to fish for survival; we fish because we simply like to eat fish. When you get that little rattle and tug on your line, you never know what's going to end up joining you in the boat. It could be a croaker, which some call a hardhead. It could be a spot or pigfish or a flounder, or maybe a bluefish or a gray trout. It could even be a swelling toad that will puff up and look like a buck-toothed softball with a two-day beard.

It matters not, and for one reason only: they're good to eat. Each, in its own way, is good to eat. And eating them is something people on Delmarva have been doing for centuries. A pigfish (*Orthopristis chrysoptera*), for example, is a beautiful little fish with subtle coloring around the gill covers ranging from orange to blue. It snorts a bit when it comes out of the water, hence the name. Few people beyond Delmarva know of pigfish, but a wonderful summer meal consists of a platter of lightly fried pigfish (head and tail left on), cornbread, fresh butterbeans and baked tomatoes. Pigfish have firm white flesh and a modestly fishy flavor, not quite as oily as spot or bluefish, not as bland as flounder.

When we go bottom fishing, we typically seek out areas that have been productive in the past. This usually means the presence of some sort of structure on the bottom: a sharp drop-off, a shell bed, a wreck, perhaps an artificial reef supplied by the state. When we lived on Onancock Creek, that meant taking the boat out to an area called Ditchbank, a few miles from the mouth of the creek. Ditchbank is an underwater river, where the depth drops from a steady twenty feet to more than fifty feet in a relatively short distance. We'd fish along the dropoff, usually in about thirty-five feet of water. We found an old shell bed along the slope, and when we anchored over it, we usually caught fish. Now and then we'd hook an ancient shell and bring it up, and in large ones we'd find small crabs, shrimp and other crustaceans. And now we know why larger fish tend to hang out on the bottom around shell beds.

Most people who live along the Chesapeake, or, for that matter, along the bays and creeks of the seaside, have favorite fishing spots such as this, places that have consistently produced nice messes of fish. When we bottom fish, we might catch croakers, gray trout, bluefish, flounder, sand mullet and, in late summer, spot and pigfish.

The fish you catch largely determines the manner in which it will be prepared. We do things with croaker, for example, that we would not do with flounder or trout. Croaker (*Micropogonias undulatus*) are what the British refer to as "coarse" fish—fitting, I suppose, in that they are caught by bottom fishing, and they are, after all, bottom feeders.

One of our favorite methods of cooking croakers is "caveman style," a cooking technique appropriate for a bottom feeder. The fish is not scaled but rather slit from vent to chin and the innards removed, and it is roasted over charcoal, spiced with salt and pepper. Scales intact, it emerges from the fire a blistered, darkened, husky wedge of fish, served in its own skin, not at all fragile and precious. A dressing of melted butter, lemon juice and seafood seasoning is drizzled over the pocket of white meat, which is gingerly pried off the bone, picked out with a fork and enjoyed with crusty bread and a cold beer.

Native Americans probably enjoyed the same dish, washed down by whatever happened to be the beverage of choice served in the bodegas of 1610.

We would never treat a flounder so coarsely. Flounder (*Paralichthys dentatus*) are fine fish with a gentle texture and flavor—some might say bland—a fish made for people who don't especially like fish, or at least fish that taste like fish. Most people fillet flounder, slicing thin, parchment-like wedges of flesh from each side of the backbone. These fillets, easily overcooked, usually end up dry and lacking flavor, needing, perhaps, a pound of fresh crabmeat for revival, which begs the question, why include the flounder?

While caveman croakers reflect a minimalist approach to preparation, flounder are worth more knifework and care. Instead of filleting the fish, we skin the flounder, leaving the large backbone intact, producing a heavy wedge of fish that will remain moist and, with some help, flavorful.

Here's how to do it: scale the fish around the outer margins on both sides. Then, using a short-bladed, sharp knife, slit just through the skin around the entire perimeter, taking care not to dig into the meat. Then, using a catfish-skinning tool or pliers, grab a corner of the skin near the head and gently pull it away from the flesh. It takes a bit of care not to pull flesh away with skin, but you'll get the hang of it. Pull the skin away on both sides of the fish, from head to tail.

With the skin removed, use the same knife to cut along the fins on both the dorsal and ventral sides. Cut at a slight angle, with the blade undercutting the small bones that anchor these fins. Use the pliers to pull the row of fins away from the fish. Cut off the head and tail and rinse the body cavity with running water. What you have now is a hunka, hunka flounder fish that will stand up to many recipes without becoming dry, tasteless and bland. The large backbone holds the fish together, helps retain moisture and is large enough not to intimidate people with aversions to fish bones. Consider it the porterhouse of fishdom.

Armed with this plank of skinned and shimmering protein, the possibilities are endless. Spice it with salt and pepper and seafood seasoning, baste it with melted butter and lemon juice and put it on the grill. With fresh flounder, less is usually more. If you must, cut a pocket between the flesh and the backbone, mix fresh crabmeat with mayonnaise and seafood seasoning and insert it in the opening. Or make a coating of mayonnaise, egg whites and lemon juice, whip them up and coat the fish. Broil it until it is done and is browned slightly round the edges.

The retail market has a great deal to do with how we perceive fish. Flounder, of course, are popular market fish, as well as desirable sport fish. They sell well in retail seafood markets and are regulars on restaurant menus along the coast. Pigfish have tended to fly under the marketing radar, and I can't recall ever seeing them advertised in a restaurant. They are not caught regularly by commercial fishermen, so they are not highly sought, except by those of us who enjoy the occasional fish fry. Pigfish and spot (*Leiostomus xanthurus*) may not be well known among the broader market, but they are very popular among Delmarva families in late summer when the corn and butterbeans are ripening, the tomatoes are heavy on the vine and that glass of sweet tea glistens in the afternoon sun.

Another wonderful fish that sees limited market share is the swelling toad (*Sphoeroides maculates*), also known as a puffer or blowfish. These fish delight kids because when removed from the water, they inflate an air bladder and become about four times their normal size. Instead of having scales, the skin is rough and coarse, similar to sandpaper. Toads might not play well in Roanoke restaurants, but many Delmarva cooks relish that slim tenderloin of white meat that lies along the backbone.

To clean toads, you slice into the skin just behind the head, pull the skin away and remove the firm, white tenderloin. Most people fry them as they would any other panfish, but our favorite recipe is toad kebabs. We use small toads, marinate them as we would shrimp and put them on

The spot is a small panfish very popular with local people.

skewers with mushrooms, pineapple chunks, sweet peppers and tomatillos or other firm vegetables. The mixture is cooked over charcoal and served with saffron rice.

Toads were not always highly regarded for their food value. When I was growing up, we would usually toss them back overboard, after tickling them to get them to puff up. And then someone discovered that tasty tenderloin.

The same is true of black drum (*pogonias cromis*), which show up in the lower Chesapeake Bay in great numbers in late spring. I recall the host of an outdoor show on television a few years ago claiming that drum were fun to catch but were inedible. Perhaps he had tried to scale and clean a large black drum and decided that the work wasn't worth the trouble. Black drum can be very large—forty to fifty pounds or more—and cleaning them can be a chore, but a smallish black drum is easy to prepare for the table and has wonderful texture and flavor. Imagine a cross between a pork loin and fish; that would be fresh drum.

A popular dish in local restaurants in May, when the drum are running, is fried drum ribs. The ribs are cut apart, with the fatty flesh left on the base of each rib. The ribs are then breaded and flash fried and served with a wedge of lemon. Like most animals, the sweetest meat on the drum is the belly of the beast, and prepared this way, it comes with its own handy handle.

Chapter 4

CLAM SIGN

Delmarva's most versatile wild food is the clam. Clams are the mother ingredient in myriad chowders. They are coarsely chopped and cooked as fritters. Clams are steamed and dipped in melted butter, mixed into batter and made into pies. Clams can be eaten raw if you're sure the water they were taken from is clean.

And that only touches the edible aspect of clams. Native Americans, ever thrifty and industrious, used to eat the flesh of the clam and then shape the shell into beads and trade them to other tribes for goods not readily available on the coast, such as stone tools.

Remember old gangster movies when a tough guy would thumb through a fistful of money and mutter, "Dat's a lotta clams"? He was talking about money, of course, and it all began here on Delmarva when an enterprising Native, a true entrepreneur, discovered that people unfamiliar with the coast fancied handsome blue beads shaped from the inner part of the clam shell. So clam shells became wampum, and when early scientists assigned genus and species names to clams, the hard clam of our coast, the source of wampum, was named *Mercenaria mercenaria*, from the Latin *mercenarius*, meaning money, or wages.

Some may consider the clam a rather homely and unexciting example of our history and culture, but clams have been part of our lives here for centuries, long before Samuel Argall discovered his "great store of fish," before Heriot described the riches of Roanoke Island, long before any blue-eyed dandy stepped out of his dinghy and sank up to his crotch in a seaside mud flat.

Even today, clams are an important part of the economy of Delmarva. Clam aquaculture is one of the fastest-growing industries in the two Virginia counties, with millions of dollars worth of cherrystone and littleneck clams shipped to restaurants and seafood markets each year. But we're not here to contemplate the economic possibilities of these native bivalves; we're here to find them, catch them, cook them and examine how this entire process is a signature of life on Delmarva. Let's go clamming.

How to Find a Clam

Clams live an inch or two beneath the surface of a tidal flat. To feed, they extend a siphon upward and pump in seawater, filtering out nutrients such as plankton and detritus. To expel waste, they use a second siphon, called an excurrent siphon, through which water and waste are pumped back to the surface of the flat.

When the tide is low and the flat is exposed, the holes left by the two connected siphons can often be seen, sometimes appearing as a keyhole shape. On Delmarva, this evidence of a buried clam is called clam sign, a phrase that can be used as a verb as well as a noun, e.g., "The clams are signing nicely today."

In theory, if you find clam sign, you're very likely to find a clam. But when it comes to clamming, as with many aspects of life, finding sign and finding a clam is not always that simple. For one thing, many creatures make holes in a tidal flat that look like clam sign. A mudflat, to the unlearned eye, seems a rather desolate landscape and not at all inviting. The flat, though, is awash with life at all tidal cycles. Dozens of species of worms drill into the surface. Snails, crabs, mussels, whelks and many other small shellfish and crustaceans burrow into the sediment. Even the birds of the flats—the willets, yellowlegs and oystercatchers—probe into the surface of the exposed flats searching for prey. So, a tidal flat is lush with life, one of the most prolific and unappreciated ecosystems of Delmarva. And yes, this complicates life for clammers. But if there were no challenge, there would be no reward.

It takes some experience to become a good signer, to learn the difference between authentic clam sign and a worm hole. And to further complicate the situation, not all clam sign looks alike. Sometimes the holes are joined in the aforementioned keyhole shape. Sometimes they are well defined, and at other times there is just the hint of a dimple in the sand. Sometimes you can find a hole with clam scat around it, providing irrefutable evidence of what lurks below. Clam scat is a tiny brown thread-like substance about one-eighth of an inch long.

If you're really lucky, you can find the hole left by the excurrent siphon, and around it will be spatter marks in the sand left by the water pumped out by the clam. This is best done on an early flood tide, after the flat has been exposed for some time at low water.

Once you've found what seems reliably to be clam sign, all that remains is to dig out the clam. On Delmarva, several tools have evolved over the years for just this purpose. A clam rake resembles a metal garden rake, but the tines are much longer. Rakes are handy for digging clams, but they are heavy and can become a burden after an hour or two on the flats. Most experienced clammers use clam picks, which have a wooden handle and a metal fork with two or three tines at the business end. If you use a pick, be sure to get one with a handle long enough to prevent you from having to bend over all day.

Not all clams are caught by signing, and not all are caught on exposed tidal flats at low tide. Many clammers wade in the shallows and use rakes to find clams buried in the bottom. My father raked more often than he signed and could fill a basket pretty quickly. He wore old sneakers to protect his feet, and he carried a wooden bushel basket that had been placed inside a tire inner tube. The inflated tube kept the basket afloat, and my father tied this clam raft to his belt with a piece of cord.

This process worked well for him for many years, until one day the wooden basket weakened after a few too many clamming trips, and as my father was lifting a basket filled with clams into the boat, the bottom gave way and the bushel of clams was suddenly scattered across the bay bottom, from whence they came. Old-fashioned hardware stores in coastal areas sell galvanized metal clam baskets, designed specifically for clamming, and my father found it wise to invest in one.

Most clams that go to market these days are aquaculture clams. That is, they began life in a laboratory and were set out in the wild after they gained some size. Prior to aquaculture, most of the clams caught were wild clams, and many of the clammers who made a profit in wild clams caught them by treading. They wore felt slippers, which protected the feet but allowed a measure of feel, and they would locate clams in shallow water simply by stepping on them. A veteran treader could dig a clam out with one foot, lift it against the opposite leg using his toes and then bend down and retrieve the clam with his hand. He usually held on to the gunwale of his clam boat while doing this to maintain balance.

Where Clams Live

Catching clams is not as simple as going out to an exposed flat at low tide and digging them out. Some flats can have many clams, while others have few or none. A flat will have numerous clams one day, none the next. Clam experts tell me that adult clams do not travel a great deal, but they do dig deeper into the flat when they sense the approach of a predator, such as a cownose ray. So, if the clams seem to have disappeared from normally productive ground, they might simply be in hiding.

Clams do have their favorite habitats, though, and if you want to find clams on a regular basis, it's a good idea to consider the clam's needs and desires. A clam wants water of the proper salinity, meaning concentrations of about 20 to 30 parts per thousand. (Ocean water is about 30 to 35 ppt.) This means that the seaside of the Delmarva Peninsula is just about ideal. The northern portions of the Chesapeake Bay are generally too brackish.

Clams want nutrient-rich plankton suspended in the water column, but they don't want clay and silt and other inorganic material that will clog up the works. The clam is not exactly a social animal, but it's crazy about sex, especially when the water temperature begins to rise in the spring. So, it wants a home where the spring warmth will nudge the mercury into the erogenous zone. Then, all the brother and sister clams will cloud the water with eggs and semen, creating a protein-rich broth that the clam community, and many others, will feed on.

The clam wants a comfortable home, a ready supply of food tastefully presented and unlimited opportunity to have sex. That's not too much to ask, I suppose. And now we know the origin of the phrase "happy as a clam."

When searching for good clamming areas, consider first the "comfortable home" portion of the equation. The clam lives just below the surface of the bottom, and it prefers a substrate it can dig into fairly easily. Mud works, as long as the water above it does not contain too much suspended material. Sand also works. But most clams prefer a combination of the two. They want a substrate that is firm enough to protect them from predators such as rays and skates, but it must be easy enough to excavate.

On a recent clamming trip, I decided to do an informal analysis of a tidal flat that was especially good clamming ground. I dug my hand into the flat, finding it firm but malleable. I worked my fingers around shell fragments and reached a depth of about four inches. I then lifted the handful of material, drained away the water and placed the remainder in a sandwich bag. The material was dark and mud-like in that it clung together when I squeezed it

Right: The clam burrows beneath the surface of the tidal flat and extends a siphon to feed and expel waste. Clammers look for the telltale key shape left by the siphon.

Below: A basket of clams is heavy. These clammers are using the clam pick to help share the load.

into a ball, but the texture was fairly rough, indicating the presence of some coarse sand and shell fragments. I took it home, put it in a dish on the picnic table on the deck and gave it a day to dry.

The dried material took on a lighter color, and when I fingered it, the grains separated like sand. As I spread it around the dish, I found a coquina in the mix, plus an oyster shell about one inch in diameter, a small mussel shell, a portion of a periwinkle and numerous other unidentifiable shell fragments.

A thirty-times hand magnifier provided a closer view. Most of the crystals were light and glass-like, probably quartz. There were a few golden ones, perhaps feldspar, and many smaller black fragments that were probably a mixture of magnetite and shell fragment. Surprisingly, there seemed to be little organic material in the mix. So, this tidal flat that is so popular with clams has virtually the same makeup as beach sand, at least in the top three or four inches. The crystals were smaller, the sand finer, but the composition was virtually the same.

This particular flat lies behind Metompkin Island, not far from a small inlet, but off the main channel that links the inlet with Folly Creek. On one side of the flat is deep water, and on the other is a salt marsh with a lush growth of cordgrass (*Spartina alterniflora*), one of the major food sources of the clam. A somewhat deeper area, perhaps eight feet wide, separates the flat from the salt marsh.

The tidal flow across the flat is constant, but not extreme, as it would be in a narrow channel. The presence of beach sand in the top layer of the flat indicates that the current does not have sufficient velocity to keep sand particles in suspension in an average tidal cycle, but there likely is velocity enough to keep lighter and smaller plankton suspended in the water, thus providing the clams their dinner.

The Spartina grasses grow tall and lush in summer, turn brown in fall and in winter begin the process of decay in which the sun's energy stored in cellulose will be carried by the tides to the sandy flats, where it will give life to millions of clams and other creatures of this shallow lagoon.

So here on one of my favorite flats, the clam has perhaps an ideal geological composition for a home, the water is clean and moves properly and there are many other clams in the neighborhood to ensure survival of the species. I can't imagine clams as social animals; I can't fathom them communicating with one another, but I rarely find solitary clams. If a tidal flat has clams, it has numerous clams, rarely just one or two, unless a storm or some other factor upset the normal life cycle.

Clams need others close by in order to reproduce. Here in this clam community, food is in plentiful supply, the salinity is perfect and there are generations of clams living here, just as in a community of humans. The large clams we find are more than thirty years old, and they have probably lived their entire adult lives on this flat, within a few square meters of where they were found.

HOW TO OPEN CLAMS

I went to a watermen's festival not long ago, and one of the exhibits featured a group of workers from a seafood packinghouse demonstrating the art of opening clams. Most of the workers were women, and they would pick up a clam, rake the bill of the shell across a coarse rasp mounted on their table and then insert a sturdy knife through the opening created by the rasp. The women then worked the knife back and forth quickly, severing the clam's two adductor muscles, and the clam would open in a cascade of salt water. The entire process took only a few seconds.

My father used a similar technique. He kept a cinder block by the back porch, and when he had a mess of clams to open, he sat on the back steps with the cinder block by his side. He would scrape the bill across the block a few times, insert an oyster knife into the opening and before long the soft, orange flesh of the clam would be shimmering in a quart jar. The neighborhood cats would gather to lap up the spilled clam juice.

Another method of opening a clam is to insert a slim-bladed oyster knife just above the hinge on the back of the clam shell. This tiny spot is the only place where the shell is vulnerable. Once the blade is inserted, it is moved back and forth to sever the adductor muscles, and then the two shells can be easily separated.

The only drawback to these methods is that there is something inherently dangerous about combining knives and clam shells. I have seen too many pierced palms, and I have on occasion donated blood of my own.

The easiest and safest way to open clams is to put them in the freezer. After an hour or so, they will open with relative ease. Keep them in the freezer overnight, and by the next morning they will be open. Thaw them and add them to your favorite recipe.

The freezer method of opening clams has several advantages, in addition to safety. You will not likely encounter shell fragments in your linguine, which happens from time to time with the scrape and stick method. Also, freezing allows you to retain all of that flavorful, salty clam juice, and this can be both good and bad. Clam juice is too tasty to have it run down the drain or to be lapped up by cats. But it is very salty, which can be an issue if you or a dinner guest has high blood pressure.

Clams can also be opened by steaming, and in recipes such as clam risotto, which calls for littleneck clams in the shell, this method is perfect. The problem with steaming is that in doing so you are cooking the clam, and that wonderful juice is being diluted with the cooking water. In some recipes, this doesn't matter, but when making chowder, clam pie, linguine with clam sauce or fritters, I prefer to begin with a raw clam in its juices.

How to Cook Clams

The seaside of the peninsula is prime clamming territory, and not surprisingly, many seaside villages and seaside residents have their favorite versions of clam dishes. On the bayside, the abundant blue crab is the signature seafood of choice, the source of soups, crab cakes and many other dishes. But on the seaside, the hardshell clam, *Mercenaria mercenaria*, is king.

The most variable clam dish by far is clam chowder. There are infinite versions, some from recipes centuries old, some connected to a certain village or barrier island community, many that are considered family heirlooms. There is a popular notion, perpetuated by the companies that sell canned clam chowder, that there are two kinds of chowder: New England, which is creamy, and Manhattan, which is tomatoey. When people go into a restaurant and see clam chowder on the menu, the next question is usually, "Is it Manhattan or New England?" That question is rarely asked on the seaside of Delmarva.

There are hundreds, probably thousands, of versions of clam chowder, with the followers of each acting like flag-waving generals from tiny republics, demanding to be heard and recognized. It goes far beyond creamy versus tomato-based.

On the Virginia coast, one of the favorites is called Hog Island Clam Chowder, a recipe that dates back to the village of Broadwater, which until the 1930s was a thriving island village of some two hundred souls. Broadwater succumbed to a rising sea level, and many of the homes and stores were barged to the mainland, but Hog Island chowder lives on, served with pride by local residents who have family ties to the island.

Hog Island Clam Chowder is a simple concoction of fresh, coarsely chopped clams, potatoes fried in bacon grease and a few onions and a few chopped tomatoes. The tomatoes are kept to a minimum, however; this is not a "tomato-based" chowder.

Purists insist that a true "Eastern Shore" clam chowder should consist only of potatoes, chopped clams with their juice and a little black pepper. A tomato never befouls this chowder, nor does cream.

Most clam chowder recipes begin with a combination of clams, potatoes and onions. Beyond that, anything goes. I enjoy linguine with clam sauce, which goes heavy on the garlic, and I see nothing wrong with introducing a few cloves to my chowder. A hint of ground mace, often used in clam pie, can be a nice touch in chowder. When the corn is ripening in July and August, I'll shave a few kernels off the ears and add them to the chowder, sweetening it nicely. A dollop of half-and-half doesn't hurt either.

One thing you don't need to add is salt. Seaside clams come with more than sufficient sodium. I once made clam sauce for linguine, using the natural juice of the clam, and cooked it down until it thickened. It was salty to the point of being inedible; I now use a little unsalted fish or chicken stock or white wine to dilute the clam juice.

As with most fresh and natural ingredients, clams usually respond best to a light touch in the kitchen. Less is more, the old adage goes. I've seen old-time clammers, on lunch break, open a dozen examples of the morning catch and have them with saltines and iced tea. "I can feel his heart beat on my tongue," a clammer once told me.

The problem with eating raw clams is that clams are filter feeders, and unless you know that the water they were taken from is clean, you stand a very good chance of picking up a nasty illness. Local health departments monitor waterways for contaminants such as fecal coliform bacteria, but when you buy clams on the open market, you have no guarantee where they came from.

Along the coast, one of the favorite ways of eating clams is having them steamed open and dipped in a little melted butter. The clams used for steaming are small. Littlenecks have a diameter of about an inch and a half. Cherrystones are somewhat larger. Both are wonderful when steamed, tender and flavorful, with a salty bite that reminds you of the seaside.

Larger clams are a bit tough for steaming but are perfect for making clam fritters, chowder, clam pie and clam sauce to go with pasta. Purists argue that clams should be chopped coarsely with a chef's knife, never minced in a food processor. I once agreed, but I've found that I can chop them perfectly in a food processor if I don't overdo it. Just a few pulses are all that's needed, with careful monitoring between pulses.

People who live near the coast are familiar with recipes using fresh clams recently removed from the shell. These would include steamed clams, linguine with clam sauce, fried whole clams, clam fritters, clam pie and clam chowder. Travel inland a bit and mention clams, and people think of clam strips and canned clam chowder. In most cases, these are made from surf or sea clams, *Spissula solidissima*, or the ocean clam, *Arctica islandica*. These are large clams that live in offshore waters. They are dredged by oceangoing vessels, shipped to mainland processing plants and then frozen and sent to food processors that turn them into chowder or breaded strips for deep frying.

I do not mean to disparage offshore clams, and I realize that *Mercenaria* are difficult to come by in, let's say, Toledo, so I would not want to deny Toledoans their processed strips and chowder at the Friday evening seafood buffet. I wish, however, that I could favor each of them with a dozen littlenecks with butter, followed by a bowl of Cedar Island Clam Chowder made from clams taken from a tidal flat about an hour before dinner.

A Few Clam Recipes

What follows are a few clam recipes, some of which our family has used over the years, some contributed by friends and a few that came from an old cookbook and predate the Civil War. When you look at the big picture, the way we find, catch and cook clams has really not changed much over the years.

One thing to be mindful of when cooking clams is that clams are a shellfish, and like all shellfish I'm familiar with, they don't respond well to over-cooking. Cook your clam chowder too long and you'll have something akin to a salty broth with pencil erasers in it. Clams need to be cooked just long enough to kill any bacteria that could possibly be present; otherwise they will be tough and rubbery. Boiling them for ten minutes should do the trick.

Hog Island Clam Chowder

2 slices bacon
6 medium potatoes, peeled and cubed
1 medium onion, coarsely chopped
1 ripe tomato, peeled and chopped
15–18 large chowder clams with juice
half-and-half (optional)

Fry the bacon in a Dutch oven until crisp. Remove bacon and chop it coarsely.

Fry the potatoes and onion in the bacon drippings until they begin to brown and a glaze forms on the bottom of the pan.

Deglaze the pan with the clam juice. I usually add some water or chicken stock to the clam juice because seaside clams are very salty. I also sometimes use a little white wine or marsala. I know this is not Hog Island style, but it tastes good just the same.

Cook until the potatoes soften and the chowder thickens. Press a potato masher into the chowder a few times to help thicken it.

Chop the tomato and add that.

With the chowder boiling, add the clams and cook for about 10 minutes, until the clams are done but not tough.

Serve in a bowl and garnish with the chopped bacon. I like to add a little half-and-half at the end to richen the chowder.

Cedar Island Clam Chowder

6 medium potatoes, peeled and cubed
1 medium onion, chopped
about 1 tablespoon bacon grease
4–6 cloves garlic
1 cup low-fat chicken stock
1 carrot
ground black pepper to taste
few sprigs fresh parsley
ground mace

15–18 large chowder clams with juice
1 cup half-and-half

Sauté the cubed potatoes and onion in the bacon grease until a glaze forms on the bottom of the pan and the potatoes and onion are lightly browned.

Chop the garlic and lightly brown it with the potatoes and onion.

Deglaze the pan with clam juice and chicken stock.

Shred the carrot and add to the chowder with black pepper, parsley and a dash of mace.

Let simmer until potatoes are done and chowder has thickened. You might want to mash the potatoes slightly to help thicken the liquid.

Add coarsely chopped clams and cook for about 10 minutes.

Add a cup of half-and-half, stir and serve.

Linguine with Clam Sauce

3 or 4 cloves garlic, chopped
1 tablespoon olive oil
about a dozen large clams, coarsely chopped, with liquid
linguine
black pepper
fresh parsley

Sauté garlic in olive oil until golden.

Add chopped clams with liquid and cook until clams are done, about 15 minutes.

Meanwhile, prepare pasta according to instructions on container.

Add pepper to taste.

Chop parsley and sprinkle over clam sauce.

Spoon sauce over linguine and serve with garlic bread or bruschetta.

Note: This recipe uses clam liquid and will be quite salty. To reduce the salt content, replace half of the clam juice with low-fat, low-salt chicken stock.

Clam Fritters

Courtesy of Terry Swain, Onancock, Virginia

12–18 large clams, shucked and coarsely chopped
black pepper
1 egg
½ cup flour
1½ teaspoons baking powder
½ teaspoon baking soda
1 medium onion, diced
cooking oil

Mix well the first seven ingredients.

Heat about ½ inch oil in skillet.

Spoon mixture into hot oil to make fritters about 4 inches in diameter.

Cook on one side until golden brown, then turn.

Drain fritters on paper towels before serving.

Clam Pie

about a dozen large clams, opened and chopped coarsely
1 egg
3 tablespoons evaporated milk
1 cup bread crumbs
1 medium onion, chopped
1 teaspoon Worcestershire sauce
2 tablespoons melted butter
¼ green bell pepper, chopped

Preheat oven to 400 degrees Fahrenheit.

Mix the above ingredients and pour into a lightly greased pie plate.

Bake for about 30 minutes.

Folly Creek Clam Pie

2 medium potatoes, cubed
1 stalk celery, chopped
1 carrot, grated
1 cup low-fat, low-salt chicken stock
2 tablespoons fresh parsley, chopped
6 ounces evaporated milk
black pepper
ground mace
1 tablespoon butter
2 tablespoons flour
2 frozen pie crusts
12–15 large clams with juice, opened and coarsely chopped

Cook potatoes, celery and carrots in clam juice and chicken stock until done, adding water if necessary to cover.

Add parsley, milk, black pepper to taste and a dash of mace, and make a roux with the butter and flour and add it to the mixture to thicken.

Simmer 10 to 15 minutes to reduce volume.

While liquid is cooking, thaw the pie crusts and place one in the bottom of a glass pie plate.

Add chopped clams to the potato mixture and cook until done, about 10 minutes.

Use a slotted spoon to transfer the mixture to the pie plate. Save excess liquid to use as gravy.

Place second crust on top of filled pie plate, tucking edges of the top layer under edges of the bottom layer. Seal edges by pressing them together with a fork. Use a knife to cut four 1-inch vents in top crust.

Bake at 425 degrees Fahrenheit for 15 minutes, then reduce heat to 350 and bake for 25 additional minutes or until crust is golden brown.

Clams Risotto

1 package risotto rice
low-fat chicken stock
1 tablespoon olive oil
a few drops dark sesame oil
about a dozen large clams, opened and coarsely chopped
12 medium shrimp, peeled
2 medium calamari, cleaned, rinsed and cut into ¼-inch rings
½ cup sherry
1 teaspoon each curry and Adobo seasoning
ground black pepper to taste
18 littleneck clams
2 tablespoons roasted red pepper
about 2 tablespoons fresh parsley, chopped
parmesan cheese
about 2 tablespoons low-fat sour cream

Prepare risotto according to package directions using chicken stock instead of water.

While the risotto is cooking, heat olive oil with a few drops of sesame oil in a heavy skillet. Add chopped clams, shrimp and calamari and sauté over medium-high heat.

Add sherry, curry powder, Adobo, ground black pepper and littleneck clams.

Cover and heat until seafood is cooked through and clams have opened, about 10 minutes.

Add coarsely chopped roasted red pepper and chopped fresh parsley and sprinkle with parmesan-romano cheese

Remove from heat, add sour cream, stir until uniform and serve over risotto.

Note: Various types of seafood can be used with this recipe. The shrimp can be replaced with scallops. Crabmeat can be added. And a can of smoked oysters will add a new twist to the flavor. We serve the risotto in a shallow bowl, sometimes making a ring around the edges of the bowl with the risotto and adding black beans in the center. The seafood mixture is poured over beans and risotto. If you use canned black beans, rinse them in a colander before serving and season them with a little cumin and/or honey mustard barbecue sauce.

Clams According to Bessie Gunter

In 1889, Bessie E. Gunter, a member of a prominent Accomack County family on Virginia's Eastern Shore, published a book titled *Housekeeper's Companion*, which became popularly known as the "Bessie Gunter cookbook." The book today is highly sought by collectors, not only because of its rarity, but also because the heirloom recipes give us a glimpse at how people prepared food in the Civil War era and before.

Recipes in the book are those of the author and eighty-nine other contributors. The book was a fundraiser for Drummondtown Baptist Church. Not surprisingly, there are many recipes for oysters, clams, terrapin, fish, crabs and other seafood. Here are two especially interesting clam recipes from the Bessie Gunter cookbook.

Clam Chowder

Mrs. Thos. E.C. Custis, Onancock, Virginia

30 clams, opened and chopped fine
2 nice size potatoes cut in blocks
a slice of pork, cut as the potatoes
1 pint of tomatoes
an onion cut fine
½ pint milk or cream
butter the size of an egg
pepper

Put the first five ingredients on to cook in about a pint of water.

Boil a half-hour or longer, then add a little pepper, half a pint of milk, a piece of butter the size of an egg, or a little cream.

Don't let it boil too dry, but let it be the consistency of vegetable soup when done.

Season with a little thyme and serve hot.

Scalloped Clams

Miss Corson, no address given

3 dozen large hardshell clams
1 medium onion, peeled and chopped
2 tablespoons butter
2 tablespoons flour
1 cup milk or cream
¼ teaspoon nutmeg
as much cayenne pepper as can be taken up on the point of a small knife blade
6 egg yolks

Wash the shells of the 3 dozen clams and put them over the fire in a sauce pan with a close cover until the shells open.

Fry the onion in the butter until it is light brown.

Remove the clams from the shells and chop fine.

When the onion is light brown, add the flour, then the clams and the milk or cream.

Season with the nutmeg and cayenne pepper.

Stew the clams gently for half an hour.

Meanwhile, arrange the washed clam shells on a dripping pan.

When the clams are done, remove the sauce pan from the fire, stir in the yolks of six raw eggs, and put this mixture into the clam shells.

Set them in a very hot oven until they are slightly browned, and serve them very hot.

Note: You can experiment with this Civil War–era recipe by adding various toppings before browning the clams. I've made it with crumbled bacon or prosciutto on top and with a topping of chopped spinach and feta cheese.

Chapter 5

CRAB POTS AND CHICKEN NECKS

There is something elemental about gathering one's own dinner. On Delmarva, hunting and fishing are noteworthy traditions. There is nothing quite like having fresh rockfish baked with potatoes and onions, sweetened with a dollop of butter and cream. Or a wintertime supper might consist of venison tenderloin sautéed with tart apples and black walnuts in a red wine reduction. Or how about black duck slow-cooked in an orange sauce, served with sweet potatoes and turnip greens spiked with peppered vinegar.

These are Delmarva dining traditions based on our kinship with the countless forests, creeks, bays, streams and guts that define our peninsula. The land and the water have fed us well.

Another aspect of hunting and gathering is even more elemental, and this would be chicken necking. Fishing usually requires a boat and a good deal of tackle. Hunting is a fine sport, but one needs guns and ammo, licenses and other gear, not to mention a place to hunt and the time to devote to planning and preparation. You can seldom just head out the door and come back an hour later with dinner.

Not so chicken necking. Chicken necking is the time-honored Delmarva pastime of recreational crabbing. Not surprisingly, a raw chicken neck is used as bait, and when the crab takes a bite, it is brought up from the bottom, scooped up in a net and placed in a pail. When crabs sufficient for dinner fill the pail, you take them home and steam them, pick out the flaky white meat and enjoy one of the best dining experiences Delmarva has to offer.

I especially enjoy two aspects of chicken necking. First, it is a primal sport, one virtually unchanged since the Nanticokes stalked these same creeks and guts, armed with no more than a piece of bait and a net. You can't get much more basic than that. Second, the meat of the Chesapeake Bay blue crab is probably the finest that a crustacean has to offer. Steam the crabs, pluck that meat free of the shell, dip it in a bit of butter seasoned with Old Bay and you're in for a memorable dining experience. The wonderful thing about blue crabs is that the less you fuss over them, the better they taste. Professional chefs go through all sorts of gyrations to make gourmet crab dishes, but with Delmarva blue crabs, less is more. Cook the crab. Eat the meat. Not exactly complicated, is it?

Delmarva has countless places to go chicken necking. Find a rural two-lane bridge that crosses a little tidal gut, and on a summer weekend there will likely be a half dozen chicken neckers hunched over the railing, one holding a string and another a net.

If you're worried about trespassing on private property, do your chicken necking at a public place, such as Assateague Island National Seashore on the Maryland end of Assateague Island. The National Park Service folks actually encourage such activity and have built a boardwalk along a bayside marsh to make crabbing easy. Signs point out the crabbing area, provide helpful tips and spell out the minimum regulations, e.g. the minimum size for jimmie (male) crabs is five inches from point to point on the shell. You can also go clamming at Assateague if you're interested in a seafood smorgasbord.

Chicken necking is a great sport for children, a tasty way to indoctrinate young people in the art of hunting and gathering. Go to Assateague on a summer day, and the boardwalk will be lined with kids of all ages, some holding chicken necks on a string, their partners armed with a net to scoop up the unsuspecting crab. Teamwork is held in high regard here.

Many local families keep a supply of chicken necks in the freezer just for the purpose of catching crabs. If we're having fried chicken, the breasts and the legs go into the pan, and the neck goes into the freezer bag. When it's time to go crabbing, the necks are thawed, a stout length of string is tied tightly around one and it is dangled from a bridge or boardwalk into the water. When a crab decides to take a taste, it usually is wise to let it settle down to feed, and when it is fully immersed in its meal, slowly lift the crab to the surface where your partner can net it. If you're on your own, it takes only a little practice to get the hang of lifting with one hand, netting with the other.

Once young people get the hang of catching crabs, it is easy to extend that interest to the life cycle of crabs and the role they play in the bays, creeks and salt marshes of the coast. For example, begin by determining whether a crab is male or female. The easiest way to do this is to look at the "apron" on the underside of the crab. The apron on the male is in the shape of an inverted *T*. A young female will have a triangular apron, and a mature female's apron will be rounded, like a shield. A female crab ready to spawn will have a mass of orange eggs under the apron and is called a sponge crab.

A single female crab will release millions of eggs each season, but few of these will survive to become adult crabs. Most will be eaten by various predators in the egg stage or as larval crabs. They nourish fish such as striped bass, croaker, eels, spot and catfish. Crabs that survive to adulthood are omnivorous eaters, feasting on small fish, shellfish, worms, crustaceans and even dead animals and plants.

Crabs are perhaps the signature hunter-gatherers of the estuary, at once predators and vultures. They are quick, ruthless hunters that will attack most anything that moves, and they are accomplished scavengers, with a ready appetite for dead animal and plant matter. For the hunter-gatherers among us who search the salt marshes and tidal waters for our dinner, we cannot help but admire them. They are an important part of our landscape, our culture, our economy.

Beautiful Swimmers

William Warner, in his seminal book on the blue crab, *Beautiful Swimmers* (Atlantic Monthly Press, 1976), wrote that the Atlantic blue crab is known to scientists as *Callinectes sapidus* Rathbun and is very appropriately named. *Callinectes* means beautiful swimmer, and *sapidus* means tasty or savory in Latin. Rathbun refers to Dr. Mary Jane Rathbun, a contemporary of Warner's at the Smithsonian Institution, who gave the crab its specific name.

Some might argue with the *Callinectes* qualities of the blue crab. It can be a fearsome-looking creature when threatened, standing high on its walking legs, stalked eyes fully extended, claws waving menacingly. It's enough to give a killifish a nightmare.

But no one argues against the *sapidus* description. The blue crab has a clean, delicate flavor, unlike fish, a quality all its own. Go to a seafood market and buy a pound of fresh backfin, or jumbo lump if you're feeling flush.

Less is often more when preparing fresh crab. This jumbo lump meat will be mixed with a sauce of mayonnaise, ketchup, horseradish and finely chopped celery.

If you're lucky, you'll get there just after the crabs have been steamed and picked and still warm from the cooker. Pry off the plastic lid and gingerly pick out a nice white lump of warm crab and pop it into your mouth. And now you know why the less you do with that crab once you get it in the kitchen, the better it will be.

Blue crabs are found all over Delmarva, from the shores of Delaware Bay southward down the string of barrier islands that line the Maryland and Virginia coast, around the Virginia Capes and northward up the bay, scattering into unknown numbers of rivers and creeks and tidal pools wherever salt water is found. Most people who live on the water keep a crab pot or two around, and when the season starts in early April, they'll bait up with a few menhaden if they have them or discards from the seafood store if they don't, and before you know it, they'll be inviting friends over for a crab steam.

When I was twenty or so, my friends and I would take the boat out to a sandy point near the mouth of a creek. We'd take along the steaming pot, some crab nets and a little Old Bay seasoning. We would beach the boat, grab the nets and then begin stalking the grass beds in shallow water looking for crabs. Meanwhile, someone would collect driftwood and get a fire going on the beach and have the steaming pot ready by the time we got back with a few dozen jimmies. There is something honest and basic about gathering and cooking your food over a fire built on the sand.

For us, catching and cooking crabs made for an entertaining afternoon, but for many people who live along the coast, crabbing is a way of life. If you spend some time in communities around the Chesapeake Bay and Delaware Bay, it becomes apparent how closely linked their lives are to the natural environment they inhabit. Take a trip to Tangier and Smith Islands, Crisfield, Deal Island, Tilghman Island or Leipsic on the Delaware Bay. Crabbing is part of the history and culture.

Richard Wong, a biometrician with the Delaware Department of Natural Resources and Environmental Control, spoke about the cultural aspects of crabs in the *Delaware State News*. "It's a summer tradition for thousands of Delawarean families—including mine," he said. "We'll get a bushel of crabs and sit at the table together and crack and pick them. It's an indulgence that brings families and friends together. Crabs are a very social meal. Typically, the biggest fishery in a state will have a big cultural impact like that on its people—for many, it's providing a livelihood."

And the good news is that the numbers of crabs are at historical highs, thanks to a reduction in pollution, harvest controls and a resurgence of the submerged aquatic vegetation needed for larval crabs. The annual winter dredge survey of the Chesapeake Bay in 2019 indicated a population of 594 million crabs, with an annual harvest of 55 million pounds. The survey is a joint effort of the Maryland Department of Natural Resources and the Virginia Institute of Marine Science. Numbers in Delaware Bay also are up, according to Wong, who noted that the estimated population in the bay is 200 million crabs, with a harvest of 4 million pounds annually.

The business of catching, processing and shipping crabs historically involved the entire community. The men in waterfront communities caught the crabs and delivered them to processing houses, where they would be cooked in large steaming vats and then picked by women and packaged into one-pound containers. The meat would be graded and priced according to quality. Jumbo lump would contain large chunks of white meat and would be the most expensive; backfin would have smaller pieces; and claw would contain only the meat from the crab's two claws. This cheaper alternative is often used in crab soup. The darker meat of the claw has a stronger flavor and texture that holds up well in soup.

There once were many crab picking houses in communities around the two bays, but today, most of the work is concentrated in fewer large facilities.

The crab picking houses were an important part of the community. The crabs were picked mostly by Black women, who would sit at stainless steel tables with their picking knives as steaming red crabs would be dumped in front of them. Early in my newspaper days, I visited the crab picking house of Eastern Shore Seafood, near Onancock, Virginia, which would employ some two dozen pickers during the heart of the season. The women who picked the crabs knew one another well and had worked together for years. In some cases, there were second- and even third-generation pickers. When the crabs were dumped onto the table and scattered around to the pickers, the women would begin their work and the room would fall silent, except for the clicking and tapping of hands dismantling crabs. Soon the work would take on a quiet rhythm, and one of the women would begin to hum, and then another, and another. And soon all of the women would be singing an old spiritual, the uplifting sound of praise in a room filled with the sweet aroma of cooked crab.

Some Crab Recipes

As I mentioned earlier, when cooking crab, less is usually more. Give me a pound of fresh lump and a fork, and I'm good to go. But on our peninsula, crabs are also a celebration of life, and when we celebrate, we need something more than a lump with a fork in it. One of the simplest and best ways I've found to dress up crabmeat came from a recipe in an old church cookbook. We call it Baptist church dressing. It's a combination of mayonnaise (we use Duke's), horseradish, ketchup and finely chopped celery. It calls for two tablespoons of mayo, one each of horseradish and ketchup and one stalk of finely chopped celery, with accent on the finely. Just mix it all up and carefully fold it into the crabmeat, and you'll have a crab salad worth saying grace over. The mixture of horseradish, mayo and ketchup perfectly complement the flavor of the crab, and the celery provides a foil to the silky texture of the crab.

We use Baptist church dressing on fish dishes as well. We especially like it on leftover salmon that has been smoked or cooked over charcoal. We like to cook salmon indirectly over coals topped with moist applewood chips tucked into a foil packet. We put a small container (i.e., an empty tuna fish can) of water under the salmon to keep it moist and cook the salmon covered for forty-five minutes to an hour, depending on thickness. We enjoy the salmon warm, with perhaps corn on the cob and new potatoes from the garden, and

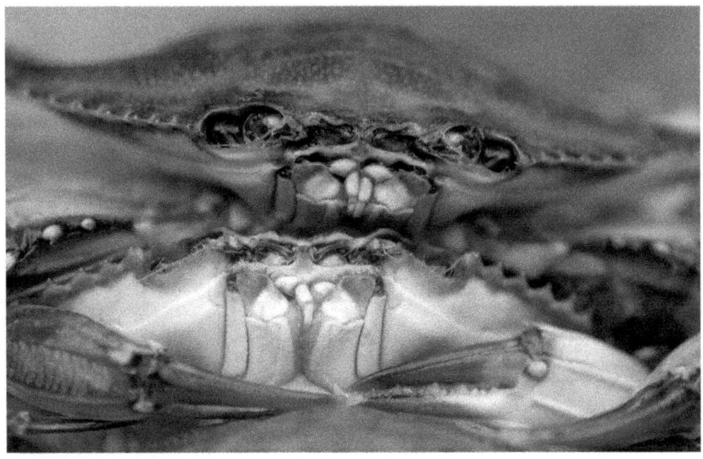

Softshell crabs are taken just after shedding, while the new shell is soft and pliable.

we save the leftover salmon to make salad, using Baptist church dressing. Amen to that.

Soft crabs are also a local delicacy. Watermen catch the crabs when they are just about to shed, and they place the crabs in a float until the old shell comes off and the new one beneath it is soft and papery. The soft crabs are fried, and soft crab sandwiches are a summer favorite in local restaurants.

Crabmeat Casserole

1 pound crabmeat
¼ cup mayonnaise
¼ cup sour cream
½ cup grated parmesan cheese, divided
¼ cup sharp or smoked cheese, grated
¼ cup red onion, finely chopped
juice of 1 lemon
2 boiled eggs, chopped
2 tablespoons fresh parsley, halved
Old Bay seasoning to taste
salt and pepper to taste

Mix the above ingredients in a large bowl, saving half the parmesan and half the parsley.

Pour into a greased baking dish and sprinkle the remaining parmesan and parsley on top.

Bake at 350 degrees Fahrenheit for 30 minutes.

Chesapeake Bay Crab Soup

1 medium onion, chopped fine
1 celery stalk, chopped fine
1 carrot, chopped medium
2 small red-skin potatoes, chopped medium
½ cup Marsala
1 cup Very Veggie (spicy) or V8
2 ripe, medium tomatoes, or frozen or canned tomatoes, chopped medium
kernels from 2 ears of fresh corn, or canned or frozen corn
small package green beans, or fresh if you have them, cut in ½-inch pieces
1 cup fish or chicken stock
2 tablespoons Old Bay
1 pound crabmeat, backfin and/or claw

Sweat the onion, celery, carrot and potato in a little olive oil in a cast-iron Dutch oven.

When those are soft, deglaze the pan with Marsala and Very Veggie, then add the other ingredients except for the crab. Add water and stock as needed.

Cook until the vegetables are done but not falling apart.

Fold in the crab. Stir to incorporate evenly in the soup, but try not to break up the large pieces.

Cook until the crab is heated through, about 10 minutes.

Note: Crab soup is a tradition along our bay shores just as clam chowder is on the seaside. Many families who live along the Chesapeake and Delaware Bays have their favorite recipes and ingredients. Some add rice to the soup; others use bacon, okra and other different vegetables. It's a good idea to simply use whatever is fresh, local and available. The two standards are the crabmeat, either lump, backfin or claw, or a combination thereof, and Old Bay seasoning. I like to use Knudson's organic Very Veggie juice in crab soup. They make a spicy blend that goes well with this recipe, or you can use old reliable V-8 and add a squirt of Sriracha chili sauce. Remember, these juices have a great deal of salt, so taste test before adding additional salt.

⁂⁂⁂

Spinach Crabmeat Casserole

6 tablespoons butter
1 cup chopped onions
¼ cup chopped green onions
2 10-ounce packages frozen chopped spinach, thawed and drained
1 pint sour cream
½ cup freshly grated parmesan cheese
2 6-ounce jars artichoke hearts, quartered and drained
½ teaspoons salt
pepper to taste
1 teaspoon Worcestershire sauce
¼ teaspoon hot sauce
1 pound crabmeat
½ pound medium-size shrimp, boiled, peeled, de-veined

Preheat oven to 350 degrees Fahrenheit.

In a large skillet or Dutch oven, melt butter and add onions and sauté until they are tender but not browned.

Add spinach, sour cream and cheese and simmer until heated through.

Add artichoke hearts, salt, pepper, Worcestershire and hot sauce and simmer 2 to 3 minutes while stirring.

Gently fold in the crabmeat and shrimp, then pour or spoon into a 2-quart casserole dish. Bake for 30 minutes.

Note: This recipe is a good method of freezing fresh crabmeat. Instead of using a single large casserole dish, use several smaller foil loaf pans or casserole pans that would provide a single serving. Reduce the cooking time to 20 minutes. When cool, wrap each pan with heavy foil, place in a freezer bag and freeze. Thaw before reheating. Leftovers from this recipe make a great cold dip or a spread for a warm English muffin.

Pan-Fried Softshell Crabs

Lynn Badger

6 softshell crabs, cleaned
¾ cup flour
1 tablespoon cornstarch
1 ½ cups vegetable oil
Old Bay seasoning
salt and pepper

Heat oil in nonstick frying pan to 350 degrees Fahrenheit.

While the oil is heating, combine flour, cornstarch, salt, pepper and ½ teaspoon Old Bay in small bowl.

Pat crabs dry and stick a sharp fork in the claws to drain water—the crabs will splatter in the hot oil otherwise.

Dredge crabs in flour mixture and sprinkle with Old Bay.

Carefully add crabs to hot oil and fry on each side for 3 to 4 minutes.

Serve with lemon or your favorite cocktail sauce. Serves 2–3 people.

Note: Most seafood stores sell their soft crabs already cleaned. But if you are lucky enough to get them whole and alive, here is how to clean them: Use kitchen shears to cut ½ inch off the front of the crab. This will remove the eyes and mouth parts. Then lift the top shell from each side and snip off the gills. Rinse the crab with cool water.

SECTION II

We Hunt, We Gather

Chapter 1

GOING GUNNING

Going gunning is a lot like bottom fishing. When you go out with the rod and reel, you're simply seeking a nice mess of fish, species and quantity unknown. Going gunning is equally nonspecific and unfocused. On Delmarva, it could mean bringing home a few squirrels, a rabbit, maybe a bird or two. You grab the shotgun, the hunting vest, stuff the pockets with a few shells of varying shot sizes and you're off. If a dog is with you, it probably is as unfocused as the act of gunning itself. It might not be a purebred bird dog, but rather a mix, a veteran of the woods that is adept at flushing and retrieving, a dog that is biddable, that will hunt close.

Gunning is unlike other field sports, such as ducking, which means you're going to the blind with the decoys before dawn and hoping to return by lunchtime with a pair of black ducks. It is unlike bird hunting, which implicitly refers to bobwhite quail and pointers and setters, or rabbit hunting, which calls for beagles. And it is not like marsh henning, which means poling a skiff through the marsh during very high tides to flush clapper rail.

Going gunning is at the core of the hunting, gathering, foraging tradition of Delmarva, and for generations it has existed to put food on the table, like catching a nice mess of fish. Ducking is a sport, a complex occupation filled with all sorts of rites and rituals, a Masonic meeting in the salt marsh. Bird hunting can be elitist. Even years ago, it involved expensive dogs, horses, professional trainers and shotguns with gold inlays. Rabbit hunting is a specialty sport, practiced by a devoted few willing to house and feed a pack of dogs all year for a season that lasts only a few weeks out of the fifty-two.

When you're going gunning, a retriever such as this black Labrador can be a good hunting partner.

Marsh henning is an accidental sport, happenstance, usually unplanned, available only when the lunar tides conspire with the daily weather to produce tides well above normal.

Gunning takes us back to our roots, before the days of game regulations, when free plunder was the law of the land. In the early nineteenth century, and well before, humans were a part of the natural system on Delmarva. We were predators and gatherers, we were omnivores, unapologetically opportunistic. Certainly, our great-great-granddaddies had farms and gardens, our great-great-grandmommas raised chickens and knew how to butcher hogs and make sausage and scrapple. But before there were game laws, we had a much more intimate relationship with the land and with the fish and the fowl and the beasts that shared it with us.

In general, we ate what was local and readily available, and the great salt marshes that surround Delmarva served as our source for most of it, our natural larder. In spring, we shot or trapped shorebirds as they migrated through. These might have included red knots that foraged on barrier beaches, dowitchers, marbled godwits, willets and other birds of the tidal flats. We went egging, foraging the marsh for the eggs of willets, gulls, clapper rails and other nesting birds. Some of the place names in our marshes still reflect this practice; Egging Marsh is east of the community of Quinby in Accomack County.

Summer was fishing season, and numerous species were eaten, with the most valuable shipped to market. We caught and ate clams, crabs, whelk and terrapin. When fall arrived, we began laying things by—fish salted in old stone crocks or put away in icehouses—and then we caught oysters for market and for the table, and by then the ducks would be plentiful. We ate them, we guided hunters from the city who killed them for sport, and through this process emerged the eminent folk art of the coast: decoy carving. These wooden birds began as functional objects, intended to lure passing birds to gun range, and now the best examples are in museums, a precious few valued at $100,000 or more.

In those days, gathering food from the natural landscape was not a sport but a way of living, a carryover from the early days of the European settlers, when a fisherman's skill meant the difference between life and death. In the eighteenth and early nineteenth centuries, few people caught fish and killed wild game to fend off starvation, but when nature provided, it was not provident to turn one's back.

Alexander Hunter was a writer from Northern Virginia who contributed to many of the leading sporting magazines of the late 1800s. Hunter spent a

Brant in flight in a seaside marsh.

great deal of time hunting, fishing and exploring the islands of the Virginia and North Carolina coast, and in 1908, he published an anthology of his adventures called *The Huntsman in the South*. Hunter was a bit of a dandy and considered himself a notch above the common people who caught fish and game for the market or for the table. He wrote of a winter night spent in the village of Broadwater on Hog Island when a great storm sent dozens of brant crashing into the bright lens of the Hog Island lighthouse.

Brant wintered by the thousands in shallow bays that separate the barrier islands from the mainland and fed on vast beds of eelgrass. Hunter was spending some time on Hog Island waterfowl hunting and was staying in the lighthouse keeper's cottage. He was awakened around 2:00 a.m. by Charles Sterling, the lightkeeper, who told him a great flock of brant had become disoriented and was hovering by the thousands around the huge light.

The two men put on their oilskins and slowly made their way across the enclosure and up the spiral steps of the tower. From the shelter of the keeper's room, which was just under the two-hundred-foot-high light, they watched as the great flock of brant became mesmerized by the intense light.

Hunter wrote:

> *The brant, the shyest, wildest, most timid of waterfowl, were within five feet of us, but, evidently blinded by the light, they could see nothing. Some would circle around the tower, others dart by; and wonderful to relate, some would*

remain stationary in the air, their wings moving so rapidly that they were blurred like a wheel in rapid motion. I thought at the time what a tremendous power must lie in their wings to enable them to nullify the wind that the instrument inside indicated was blowing at sixty-five miles per hour.

The lamp in the tower revolved every forty-five seconds, and for a short time every bird was in the vivid glare, which displayed every graceful curve of neck and head, and the set and balance of the body, and enabled one to look into their brilliant eyes.

The brant is not a glossy, showy bird like the wood duck or mallard, but in the driving rain and under the powerful rays of the lamp they were exquisitely beautiful, their plumage looked like ebony, and the tints changed to many an iridescent hue. Every few seconds, above all the rush of the wind, would be heard a loud tinkling sound as a blinded brant, dazed by the rays, would strike the double two-inch plate glass that surrounded the burner, and fall dead from the impact; sometimes dying on the platform of the tower, but more often falling on the ground.

Charles Sterling, Hunter wrote, picked up twenty-eight dead brant, and at the base of the tower islanders and their dogs collected dozens of dead or stunned waterfowl, "the exact number they never divulged."

Hunter reacted to the actions of the local people with disdain, and his readers no doubt felt great sympathy for the unfortunate brant, but to the islanders it was a serendipitous event. When nature is your provider, it is wise to accept such gifts as they come, because such benevolence is rare. Many Broadwater families dined on roasted brant over the following days.

It seems to me the people of Hog Island represented the final chapter of Delmarva's colonial spirit. They were opportunists, and their disdain for the sporting aspects of the hunt made them ready targets for modern, fair-minded writers such as Hunter. But Hunter probably understood these island people well enough to know that their refusal to bend to social constraints and the code of law was certainly not a matter of contempt for the wildfowl.

The islanders believed strongly in independence and self-reliance, and they had overwhelming, if naive, confidence that God and Nature would provide for them, that the waterfowl would continue to come in great numbers, that the fish would always fill their nets, that the oysters would always grow fat and fertile. Perhaps no group of people had a more intimate relationship with the land and the sea and with the Creator who supplied this bounty.

As the population grew along the coast, more pressure was put on what was indeed a finite natural resource. Trade was established between the rural communities of Delmarva and cities such as Baltimore, Philadelphia, New York and Boston. Sailing ships and steamships ferried local agricultural crops to markets, and along with the potatoes and grain crops went barrels of fish, oysters, clams, terrapins and wild ducks. The opening of the railroad in the 1870s and 1880s ushered in a new era of commerce and trade.

The term *sustainable* is widely used today in conservation circles, and in the mid- to late nineteenth century it became apparent that the natural food resources of the coast could not be sustained given the market demand from growing East Coast cities. Maryland and Virginia passed laws regulating the seafood industry, and the last two decades of the nineteenth century saw the passage of the first game laws.

Alexander Hunter served in the Virginia legislature and proposed some of the early regulations. Within a few years, night shooting was outlawed, spring shooting was prohibited and wild game was given the Sabbath as a day of rest. Hunter advocated stationing a game warden on Hog Island for six months of the year.

So, our great store of fish and game had gone from becoming a matter of survival for early colonists to a state-regulated source of sport for those with

Decoy carvers Grayson Chesser and Cameron McIntyre hunting brant with handmade decoys.

leisure time and money to spend. And rural people, such as the Broadwater residents of Hog Island, were converted from God-fearing, law-abiding citizens to outlaws almost overnight by the passage of laws. The era of free plunder had ended.

The transition from survival to sport very likely had implications beyond the viability of the natural resource. During this period and earlier, the traditions and culture of the English greatly affected our food—how it was prepared, how it was presented, the manner in which it was consumed. As landowners and businessmen became prosperous, they initiated in their American homes the manners and foodways of their ancestors back in England.

These manners also extended to the field, where in England the hunt was a social event, a gathering of the elite, and certainly not a means of putting food on the table. The best hunting lands were owned or controlled by the nobility, as were the best fishing waters. Free plunder was considered gluttonous, exploitative, a reflection of a lack of breeding. The passage of hunting laws in America probably had as much to do with the enforcement of manners as it did with protecting ducks, fish and other game. Hunting and fishing were seen as sport exclusively for the elite, and there was an effort to prevent poor whites and slaves from participating in these activities.

In *The Huntsman in the South*, Hunter paints himself as the aristocratic, well-mannered sportsman who observes a certain code of ethics that sets him apart from the common people of Broadwater, who would stoop to picking up dead brant from the base of a lighthouse and taking them home for the table. We see in his writing this dichotomy of the use of natural resources. On one hand is the spirit of gunning, of indiscriminately providing food without ceremony or manners, and on the other hand is hunting as sport, and with it the rites and rituals attendant to people who have manners, who abide by a code of ethics.

Alexander Hunter, author of *The Huntsman in the South*.

Gunners and sportsmen shared Hog Island for a while, and during the years following the Civil War, the transition was clearly moving in favor of the sportsmen. As could be expected, it did not go smoothly. Hunter writes that he went to Hog Island in the early part of the season and expected fine shooting. He

A young fisherman shows off a nice flounder.

This basket of fresh clams will be turned into chowder, fritters or perhaps linguine with clam sauce.

Left: The best time to go clamming is at low tide when the tidal flats are exposed and clam sign can be seen. Clams burrow just beneath the surface and send up a siphon to feed and expel waste.

Below: The clam is sometimes considered a rather homely creature, but from the right angle, it has a form that might be considered graceful.

Clam fritters are made by coarsely chopping clams and mixing them in a batter of flour, baking powder and baking soda. They are fried in hot oil until brown and crispy.

There are many recipes for clam chowder in the coastal communities of Delmarva. This one keeps it simple: clams, potatoes browned in bacon drippings, a little onion and bacon bits. It is finished with a little half-and-half.

Fried soft crabs are a warm-weather delicacy on Delmarva. Peeler crabs are caught just before shedding, and as soon as the hard shell is discarded, they are battered and fried.

Fresh crabmeat requires little in the way of preparation. This jumbo lump is mixed with a little "Baptist church dressing" (see text) and served on a bed of greens fresh from the garden.

Right: A duck hunter sets out decoys at sunrise on a seaside marsh. Duck hunting has been a popular outdoor sport on Delmarva for generations.

Below: Rabbit hunting usually involves dogs, often beagles, that will flush and run the rabbit while the hunters wait for it to pass by them.

Left: Guide Rick Kellam poles his skiff through a salt marsh at high tide, hoping to flush a clapper rail.

Below: The clapper rail (*Rallus longirostis*) is abundant in coastal salt marshes and is frequently heard but seldom seen, preferring to hide in the vast expanses of spartina grass. They are hunted when high tides flood the marsh.

A few rails on the seat of Rick Kellam's skiff reflect the success of a morning hunt. Rails are a rare treat in coastal communities. They have a wild flavor much like upland game birds.

As the high tide recedes, Rick walks the marsh and bags a few more rails to take home to the kitchen.

A diamondback terrapin retreats to the surf of Hog Island after laying a clutch of eggs just beyond the high tide line. The terrapin population fell drastically in the early 1900s when they became popular in city restaurants. Their challenge now is finding suitable nesting areas such as this.

Many coastal residents look forward to a muskrat dinner during the winter months. These were caught by a local trapper and were for sale at Susan's Seafood in New Church, Virginia.

The majority of oysters and clams sold in local seafood shops on Delmarva today are the products of a growing aquaculture industry. These "Big Salts" in Susan's Seafood are the exception. They were wild caught.

The old, decommissioned Coast Guard station on Assateague Island is a popular landmark, one of the few island stations that remain. It was photographed from Chincoteague National Wildlife Refuge.

Left: One of the most satisfying moments for gardeners comes when potatoes are dug in early summer. New potatoes and fresh green peas are the gardener's reward for all the hard work.

Below: A popular breakfast on Delmarva in the spring is shad roe served with bacon and scrambled eggs.

Black skimmers nest on the barrier islands in spring, usually arriving in early May. They feed by skimming over the surface of a creek with their lower mandible dipping into the water. Old-time Delmarva residents called them "cut waters."

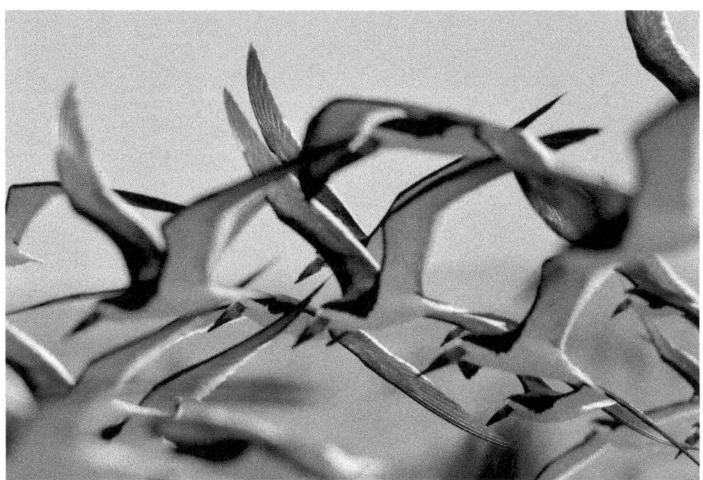

Skimmers nest in colonies beyond the high tide line on sandy beaches. They often nest with a variety of tern species and American oystercatchers.

A lone oysterman gathers wild oysters growing in a seaside marsh.

Brant winter by the thousands on the seaside of Delmarva. These were photographed just before sunset at Chincoteague National Wildlife Refuge.

The author doing research on a clam flat near Cedar Island.

The Cedar Island Coast Guard Station is on a seaside marsh east of the town of Accomac. It was decommissioned in the 1950s and is used as a private lodge today. The birds in the foreground are short-billed dowitchers.

Fig trees like the sandy soil of Delmarva, and most of us on Delmarva like fig preserves. These were peeled and cooked in a sugar solution until tender. A slice of lemon adds color and zest.

Generations ago, most Delmarva families kept orchards as well as kitchen gardens. Fig trees are still popular, mainly because you can't find figs like this in the produce section of the grocery market. If you want fig preserves, you have to grow your own or make friends with someone who does.

Boat-tailed grackles are commonplace on the seaside and are often overlooked in favor of more glamorous birds such as skimmers, whimbrels, godwits and terns. But when the light is just right and the grackles are interacting with one another, they can produce an evocative image.

These mating zebra swallowtail butterflies have created a heart-shaped image—perfect, perhaps, for a Valentine's Day card.

Strawberries were an important crop on Delmarva in the early 1900s, and there are still some growers around today. These gorgeous berries are from William Baines's farm near Eastville in Northampton County, and they taste as good as they look.

Three tundra swans are reflected in a pool at sunset on Chincoteague National Wildlife Refuge.

climbed the watchtower one evening, scanned the inlet with a scope and said the water was black with wildfowl. Early the next morning, he prepared to set out for his blind when he was told the birds had gone. A few local residents had spent the night blasting them, driving the birds away.

While there was resentment of the new regulations, some of the more enterprising residents realized a profit could be made by guiding visiting sportsmen, providing them room and board and preparing their game for shipment back to their homes. Hunting clubs were built—some very lavish, some spartan—and so began the modern era of sport hunting along the coast. Gunning was still practiced in many a seaside village or town, but it had clearly become the era of the sport. Today, one rarely hears a person speak of going gunning.

Perhaps none of the destinations was as famous in its day as the Cobb family hotel on Cobb's Island, just south of Hog Island. It was run by a Massachusetts boatbuilder named Nathan Cobb, who relocated to the peninsula in 1837. Cobb and his sons ran a lucrative ship salvage business, and they built a rambling frame hotel, advertised in the leading sporting journals of the day and attracted not only hunting parties in fall and winter but beachgoers and fishermen during the summer.

The peak years of the hotel were the two decades following the Civil War. By 1880, the patriarch of the family was in ill health and various reports indicate the hotel had fallen into disrepair. The Virginia General Assembly in 1882 approved legislation incorporating the Cobb's Island Seaside Company, the purpose of which was to purchase the island and repair the hotel. One of the principals of the company was our friend Alexander Hunter, who at the time represented the city of Alexandria in the General Assembly.

The efforts of the syndicate were apparently short-lived. The Cobb family sold the property. It passed through numerous hands, and in 1896, a series of storms destroyed most of the buildings. By 1900, any tangible sign of the Cobbs' presence on the island had disappeared.

The Cobbs' legacy lives on today through the decoys the family carved. Nathan Cobb was a talented woodworker who passed along his skills to his sons. Nathan Cobb Jr. was the most accomplished sportsman of the family and was a decoy carver of the first rank. His carvings have sold at folk art auctions for tens of thousands of dollars. Elkanah Cobb, son of Nathan Jr., was also an accomplished carver and guide. The Cobbs used native woods and basic tools and were noted for being able to capture the essence of a bird with simple, elegant lines. The Cobbs' decoys were a perfect, if rustic, example of the architectural dictum "form follows function."

Chapter 2

MARSH HENNING TIDES

My father and I were alone in a small cedar skiff, waiting for the marsh to flood. We could see the ocean break over the dunes of the barrier islands, and we could hear the violence of the open water as the offshore sandbar slowed its pace, forcing it to tumble onto the berm of the beach, white plumes of salt spray skittering across the sand.

But where we were, in a leeward marsh protected by the islands, the water was calm and silent, running in strong, deep currents through the narrow creeks that laced the salt marsh. The water rose almost imperceptibly, first covering the bases of the marsh plants, climbing slowly to the salt rim that marked the normal level of high tide and then continuing to rise, covering the shorter grasses and obscuring the winding creeks and guts, until finally there was no marsh but a flat expanse of rising water where only patches of high grass showed. The ocean inlet between the islands, the shallow bay that separated the islands and the mainland and the marshes were all as one, covered with water from the barrier island dunes to the line of trees on the distant mainland.

The moon was full, and the pull of the moon's gravity tugged the water toward the land. A northeast storm was offshore, and its winds pushed the ocean as the moon's gravity pulled, sending the breakers far up the beach, over the islands in low areas and into the marshes and the forests and fields of the mainland.

I sat on a rough board bench in the bow of the skiff, holding my father's old double-barreled shotgun across my lap, and watched the tide rise, feeling its silent power against the hull of the boat, which my father held steady in the current with a long oak push pole. I wondered about the tide. What if it were not to crest? What if it were to continue beyond the time of high water, and what if instead of soon ebbing, it continued to rise, even if only for a few hours? Already the marsh had been covered, the landscape erased, familiar benchmarks removed, all reference to solid land gone. The woods and fields would be next, and the houses and farms, the small towns and businesses, schools, churches. And I realized how our lives are governed by cycles such as the rising and falling of the tide, how we trust in the precision and predictability of natural events. Afloat on a flooding tide, I realized how precarious life is, how subject to change, how fragile and fleeting, how dependent on a process that has no margin for error.

It was September, and the northeast wind carried the first cold insinuations of winter. My father and I were alone. On the open water, there were no other boats, none for miles. I sat in the bow of the skiff and nervously fingered the double-barreled shotgun, clicking the safety switch on and off, on and off. I felt in my pockets for the shells; I shuffled them with my hand, and it made me feel warmer, shells tightly packed and heavy with powder and lead, their brass bases clicking together in a satisfying way.

A retriever can help find fallen birds.

It was time, my father said. He stood and planted the long push pole into the flooded marsh, and the boat pressed forward. He told me to load the gun, and I slid in two shells and snapped it shut, checking the safety switch. My father poled the boat along the edge of a flooded salt marsh gut. Grass grows higher on the edge of a gut because it is fed by the twice-daily flush of the tides. In the flooded marsh, wisps of green grass remained above water, defining the meandering path of the gut. My father pushed the boat through these green grass tops, and I sat in the bow with the gun, watching the grass fifty yards ahead of us, looking for the bobbing heads of clapper rails, which we called marsh hens.

My father saw the first one, which was not swimming ahead of us but off to one side, attempting to flank us and get behind us. It was in the open water, bobbing and weaving, no grass in which to hide. As I lifted the gun, the rail reluctantly flushed, its wings stirring the surface of the still water. My shot peppered the water around the bird, creating an ellipse of foam. The shot seemed startlingly loud and out of place in this marsh where the only sound was the rumble of distant waves. The marsh hen lay on its back, kicking its leg, a last gasp of muscle memory. I raised the gun to shoot again, but my father leaned forward and pressed his hand on my shoulder, and I took the gun down. He pushed the boat to the bird, and I picked it up, dead now, eyes glazing, wet but warm, much larger than I had expected, soft, all neck and legs, subtle browns and grays, tiny head and long bill.

My first bird. I must have been thirteen. *It's a good tide*, my father said, by way of congratulations.

The current had stopped flowing, and the tide crested at seven feet above mean low water. A good marsh henning tide. We had consulted the tide table the day before, knowing that the full moon would produce a tide of about six feet above mean low. But the northeaster offshore turned a marginal henning tide into an extraordinary one.

You get these tides only a few times a year, when moon phase and weather conspire to drive the tide higher than normal, covering all but the tallest grasses of the high marsh. The marsh hens, which normally have thousands of acres of tall grass in which to hide, become vulnerable for perhaps two hours, just before the crest of the tide and just after. So my father poled the boat along the grassy rim and I shot marsh hens, and then I poled the boat and my father shot, and as the morning grew old, the sun warmed us and the tide began to fall. And as the tide fell, we left the skiff and walked the high marsh, flushing rail birds from tumps of grass. By noon, we had filled our limits of fifteen birds each and started home.

The clapper rail is plentiful in the seaside marshes along the coast and also along the lower Chesapeake Bay.

My first hunting trip, a seaside baptism of full immersion, I thought, an introduction to the discomforting reality that in order for me to live, something else must die. That night, our family had marsh hens for dinner. They had a wonderful wild taste, milder than wild duck, but with the flavor of the marsh: slightly salty, slightly fishlike.

I was proud of having killed these birds, of having helped feed our family. It was the directness of the process of life and death, the unbending reality of it, that made its impression on me. My father and I went out in a flooding tide and killed food for the family, much as a hawk might, or a fox, or, for that matter, a marsh hen as it plucks a grasshopper from a blade of spartina grass. I felt, in a vague and uncertain way, that I knew nature better by having participated in it, eliminating the cattle ranches, poultry farms, slaughterhouses and grocery markets that turn the daily business of living and dying into an unseen and abstract concept. Would I have felt the same pride had I spent the morning mowing my neighbors' lawns and then taken the money to the grocery market and exchanged it for chicken

Although the rails are plentiful, they are shy birds and are seldom seen.

or steak? Is it more moral or less moral to kill your own dinner or to pay someone to do it for you?

In the salt marsh on that September morning, morality was not an issue, yet I knew that the violent act of ending a bird's life was heavy with implications. It was different from catching fish or clams, even though those acts also meant the death of a flounder or shellfish. Perhaps it was the violence and finality of the shot, the decision to pull the trigger, the letting of blood. It signified something, as in Isaac McCaslin's first worthy blood in Faulkner's *The Bear*: the symbolic abandonment of childhood, a rite of passage charged with certain indelible emotions that remain with you throughout life. After many marsh henning tides, death has not become common, not without silent reverence, thankfulness and pride—emotions I have never felt at the supermarket checkout counter.

I have come to love rail birds because they remind me that I am not above nature, but part of it. If I destroy their marsh, they will be gone, and in the rails' absence, marsh henning tides will have no relevance, no currency, and the value of my life will be just as diminished as theirs. So, the point is to protect those places that sustain rail birds in order that a few might sustain me.

Chapter 3

DIAMONDBACK TERRAPINS AND OTHER JEWELS

The diamondback terrapin is the signature reptile of Delmarva. It lives in the Chesapeake Bay, the Delaware Bay and all along the Atlantic shoreline in the spartina marshes that separate the barrier islands from the mainland. It thrives in the super-salty environment of coastal estuaries, and it is comfortable as well in the brackish rivers and creeks that flow into the bay. The diamondback is our only turtle that lives in brackish water.

The diamondback terrapin got its name from the Algonquin term *torope*, which some say means "edible turtle." It is the state reptile of Maryland, and it is the mascot of the University of Maryland sports teams. While Delmarva is known around the nation for crabs, clams and oysters, it is the diamondback terrapin that has given drama and life to our foodways. It is strictly an American animal, one that fed indigenous people for centuries and was then shared with European colonists when they arrived. It has thrived in our waters, and it once was nearly exterminated. On Delmarva, the diamondback terrapin has been both revered and reviled as it threaded its way through our food culture.

In the late 1800s and early 1900s, the terrapin was the star of city restaurants, fetching prices only the wealthy could afford. But prior to the Civil War, terrapins were plentiful and commonplace. Plantation owners provided them as food for slaves as an alternative to pork, prompting the slaves to protest. George Washington used terrapins to feed the troops at Yorktown when supplies were running low, and it was common for farmers to feed terrapins to chickens and pigs. An article on terrapins in *Forest & Stream* magazine in 1899 said that over a period of a few years, terrapins went from selling for $1 for an oxcart load to as much as $160 a dozen.

The reason, of course, is that terrapins were discovered by well-known restaurants in eastern cities, and demand skyrocketed over a relatively brief period of time. This led first to overfishing of the natural population of terrapins, and it also led to a proliferation of terrapin farms, where thousands of terrapins would be raised in captivity to satisfy the demand of the restaurant market.

And so, it would be fair to ask how a humble reptile that once was used as emergency rations for troops and provided as food for slaves achieved its celebrity status. The answer is that when Washington's enlisted troops and slaves were fed terrapins, they were likely roasted in their shells over a bed of coals. If they were lucky, the recipients might have been provided a dollop of butter for seasoning. City restaurants prepared terrapin dishes with profuse amounts of cream, butter, liquor, egg yolks and spices. If I gave you my gardening shoes and you slow-cooked them for two hours, then cut them into bite-sized pieces and prepared them according to a terrapin recipe from a late nineteenth-century cookbook, you would get a three-star rating from Michelin.

When the big-city restaurants discovered terrapins, they fell into something that had been commonly known on the Delmarva Peninsula for generations: when prepared properly, terrapins are delicious. You can find lots of terrapin recipes in old cookbooks, and most involve cream, butter and some sort of spirits. People who lived on Delmarva and in the Chesapeake Bay area had been eating terrapins for years. They were cheap, readily available and, until being discovered by the restaurant crowd, the population was strong and stable. It is probable that the railroad was at least partially liable for spreading the good news about terrapins to the north. As steamboat and railroad service extended farther and farther south in the 1870s and 1880s, travel from eastern cities to the rural Eastern Shore became relatively quick and easy. Folks from up north visited and enjoyed a fine dish of terrapin stew, and the word spread.

Terrapins were part of the culture of rural Delmarva in the post–Civil War days. They were a reason for people to get together and share food and fellowship. Benjamin Azariah Colonna was born on October 17, 1843, near Pungoteague in Accomack County, Virginia. He grew up on a farm in an area known as Pennyville, and late in his life, he wrote a narrative about terrapin suppers, which were a winter tradition in the rural farming community in the years following the Civil War. We'll let him tell his story:

> *A terrapin supper among the farmers in those days was something very different from the terrapin supper that city people know today. In the first place the terrapin itself had to be a "count." That is to say it had to be at least seven inches over the top of the shell.*
>
> *When the guests were invited they were asked whether they would like their terrapin boiled or roasted. To boil a terrapin, it was put in a pot on the stove and left until the undershell would come off easily. To roast a terrapin, it was wrapped up in white corn shucks and tied slightly and covered with hot ashes and coals, just as a sweet potato would be covered to roast it.*
>
> *The table was spread for the number of guests invited, and in front of each plate was placed salt, pepper, vinegar, and a little mustard. In the center of the table there was a large plate of fresh butter. There was always a decanter of brandy or whiskey, and an abundance of hot coffee and hot Maryland biscuits.*
>
> *The guests were seated at the table and the terrapins were brought in one at a time and placed in front of them, each man getting the kind he had asked for. When the old-fashioned country grace had been given with great fervor by one of the good people, the supper would begin. Each guest took off the undershell and opened the whole terrapin. As terrapin suppers were never given until after the terrapins had cleansed themselves for the winter, it was a very easy matter to clean them. The dry, black outer skin was loosened and removed, and the gall bladder removed. Then each man would mix up his terrapin thoroughly in the shell and season it to suit his taste and proceed to eat it with knife, fork, and spoon right out of the shell. They used liberal quantities of butter in the terrapin along with other things to suit their taste. Whiskey and coffee were passed around and the supper eaten with great gusto.*
>
> *It is useless to say that such terrapins were a great deal better than terrapin which is served now-a-days in restaurants. The delightful, delicate taste of that terrapin, and the superior quality of the terrapin itself, made it better than anything I have seen for many a year.*
>
> *As a general thing, no ladies were at the table at a terrapin supper. It was strictly a stag affair. Sometimes, some members of the party would remain at the table for hours playing cards, though they were all friends and neighbors, there was never any high betting, cheating, or falsifying. They were a pretty merry crowd when they went home at an early hour in the*

morning, to meet again at a later date at some other neighbor's house. They each gave a terrapin supper during the winter so that each man attended some seven or eight suppers during the season.

The colored people too had as many terrapins as they wanted, though as a general thing not counts, for if a colored man, in looking for a terrapin for himself, should happen upon a count, he would be mighty apt to sell it. The price of count terrapins today, even if they can be had at all, would be prohibitive to anyone but a millionaire, and as to ten men sitting around a table, each with a count before him which he would pick and serve in his own way, their host would be reduced to poverty because of their great price.

Of course, in order to have a terrapin supper it was necessary to have terrapins, and most rural people who lived on the coast were adept at finding and catching terrapins. Reading Colonna's account, the first impression is that this man is a naturalist; at least that would be the term used today. But he was simply a man living off the land, and in order to be successful, he had to know the workings of nature. Here he explains where, when and how to catch terrapins:

An expert at taking terrapin will select some quiet morning after a northwest blow, and before the water has a ripple on it will be out with his tongs looking at the bottom of the creeks. He can see the bottom as plainly as though it were exposed, for the fish and crabs have stopped running about and the water is perfectly clear. To one unaccustomed to this business, the bottom would look the same everywhere; but an experienced man will observe a number of prints on the bottom which look something like a horse's footprints. Under such a sign there will always be a terrapin, the bigger the sign, of course, the bigger the terrapin, so that a man can always tell before he puts the pincers down what size terrapin he is to get. It depends on the quietness of the water, the length of time before a ripple comes on the face of the water, and of course upon the thickness (amount) of the terrapin, as to the number that he will take in a morning. But big or little, it was not extraordinary luck to take from 50 to 80 terrapin in one morning, while with exceptionally good luck I have known them to take more than 150.

And Colonna on terrapin natural history:

In the spring of the year the terrapin seek a nice warm sandy shore to lay their eggs. They generally select the shores of the Chesapeake Bay or the

This diamondback terrapin is laying eggs on the beach of Hog Island in Northampton County.

ocean shore. They scratch a little hole in the sand and lay their eggs. The half-grown terrapin will lay more eggs than you would think a terrapin could possibly hold. The eggs are pinkish in color and have a very soft shell and I have never seen one taken from the nest that did not have a dent in it. But perhaps they are laid with the dent already in them.

The old terrapin, having covered her eggs up, will disfigure the ground for a yard or two around, so as not to make it apparent where the eggs are. She doesn't watch the nest or give herself any further concern about it but takes to the ocean immediately. When the terrapins are hatched, the little bits of things are not larger than a five-cent piece. They seem to be quite capable of taking care of themselves at once, and they swim away just as the old one did. You will find them all through the summer, from little bits of fellows to three or four inches in length. After the first year, however, the growth is very slow. It does not shed or slough its shell like the crab every time it grows. Its shell, on the contrary, grows as the terrapin grows.

Terrapin Farms

The terrapin began its transition from rural folkway to regular appearances in New York's finest restaurants around 1850. *Forest & Stream* magazine reported in its September 2, 1899 issue:

> *About fifty years ago Capt. John Etheridge sold in Norfolk about 3,000 fine diamond-backs for $400, and a little later he shipped to Baltimore about the same number, receiving something over $350. This, it is said, was the beginning of the onslaught on the terrapin, and from Cape Fear to Baltimore men engaged in the work of terrapin hunting. It is known that terrapin formerly lived in colonies, but constant dredging caused them to scatter, and from that time until the present the catch has grown smaller each year.*

As the population of wild terrapins dwindled, terrapin dealers began to raise them in captivity, usually in enclosures of a few acres of marsh and ponds. The "turtle farmers" would buy terrapins from local fishermen, store them in the enclosed area and then ship them to market in the fall and winter, which was considered terrapin season. Quite a few people who lived on the coast of Delmarva set up turtle farms, but most were modest operations that sold to a local market. Miles Hancock, the well-known decoy carver from Chincoteague, Virginia, was a terrapin farmer as well as a carver.

The largest turtle farms were in Crisfield, Maryland, where in the late 1800s, tens of thousands of terrapins were being raised for the restaurant trade. The major dealers of terrapins in Crisfield were A.R. Riggin and A.L. LaVallette, who were thought to have been the largest suppliers in the country. Dr. George W. Massamore, secretary and treasurer of the Maryland Game and Fish Protective Association, visited Crisfield in November 1897 and reported that more terrapins were being shipped from Crisfield than from all other points in the state combined. November marked the beginning of the terrapin season, and when Massamore visited A.R. Riggin's impoundment, he found more than twenty thousand terrapins. He wrote:

> *The sight was novel. I visited Mr. Riggin's pound just after the terrapins were fed. The scrambling after mashed hard crabs, upon which they were fed, was an interesting sight. The terrapins were so thick that they were crawling over each other; the pound was a moving mass that filled me with wonder and amazement. Think of 20,000 diamond back terrapins on the*

> *move at the same time, within an enclosure of about an acre. The tide was low, affording a good view. The ditches, grass tussocks and mud puddles all seemed like a living, moving, conglomerate mass, struggling for life.*

Massamore said that LaVallette was the first dealer to successfully introduce impounding terrapins as a business. He said nearly all of the terrapins caught by fishermen in the Crisfield area were sold to either LaVallette or Riggin, who also bought stock from North Carolina sources. Massamore described the terrapin impoundments as an enclosure made of "a tight board fence, ten feet high, with wire screens across the openings where the water floods and ebbs in and out. The pounds are watched day and night by armed men to protect the terrapins from being stolen."

While the Crisfield operations basically depended on stockpiling wild terrapins of various sizes and ages until they were marketable, others attempted to raise terrapins from eggs to produce a more uniform brood. Benjamin West, president of the Fulton Fish Market in New York City, built an enclosure on his farm on the Shrewsbury River in New Jersey, procured eggs and raised five thousand young terrapins, which, unfortunately, escaped from the enclosure. West said that he went out to check on the young terrapins one morning and found that they had climbed the thirty-inch wall. They were later found in his asparagus patch.

Terrapin farming worked for a few years, but when it failed, it nearly exterminated the population of diamondback terrapins. Terrapins are slow-growing animals, and they take years to reach marketable size. It simply was not feasible to raise thousands of them in a confined setting for an extended period of time. George Massamore wrote after visiting the Crisfield operations:

> *From all the information obtained during my stay in Crisfield, I am thoroughly convinced that the impounding of terrapins must necessarily result in their final extermination. It is a well-established fact that terrapins will not propagate confined in pounds. Females lay from 12 to 20 eggs twice during the season for incubation. A fair estimate for each female would be 30 eggs. Take 20,000 female terrapins now held in confinement in the pounds at Crisfield (this number I am told is a modest estimate), and the result figures up the destruction of 600,000 young terrapins. These figures demonstrate very clearly the necessity for a strict enforcement of the laws against having in possession terrapins out of season.*

States in the Chesapeake Bay area passed legislation to protect the terrapins, they slowly recovered and now it's common to paddle a canoe up a remote creek and see terrapin heads popping up around you. The greatest threat to diamondback terrapins today is loss of habitat, especially the sandy beaches that are so important to them in spring when they lay eggs. In many developed areas around the bay, sandy beaches have given way to bulkheads, rock walls and other hardened shorelines. Terrapins simply cannot nest there.

Bacchanalian Carousals

It is true, that the mortality on this Shore in bye-gone days was very great, but that, I think, was owing more to the luxurious and Epicurean style of living which then prevailed than to the climate. For now, when terrapin and oyster suppers and bacchanalian carousals have become less frequent, a very decided improvement in the health of the Peninsula has taken place.
—John H. Snead, assistant marshal of St. George's Parish, in a report for the 1850 Census of Accomack County

Nothing succeeds like excess.
—anonymous

And now we come to the good part.

Of all the grand food traditions that have passed through the kitchens of Delmarva, I most regret that I will never taste terrapin stew as it was presented at a good old-fashioned bacchanalian carousal. I regret, too, that I will never shoot shorebirds in the spring and experience the wild flavor of a robin snipe, a calico back or perhaps a Hudsonian curlew. But that's okay. I've eaten marsh hens, which remain quite legal, and that's close enough to shorebird for me.

I have an old copy of Bessie Gunter's *Housekeeper's Companion*, and thumbing through it is like making my way back through the generations. My mother owned the cookbook, and my grandmother before her. My grandmother had a modern kitchen with an electric range and all the latest conveniences, but she kept an old wood-fired cookstove down in what she called the cellar. If any serious cooking were to be done, it would involve a trip to the cellar.

The Thanksgiving turkey, the Christmas ham, the homemade biscuits and yeast rolls—all were created down in the cellar.

When I thumb through Bessie Gunter's cookbook (that's what everyone called it, not *Housekeeper's Companion*), I can smell the woodsmoke from my grandmother's cellar. I can feel the warmth hanging against the low ceiling, and I can hear the snap and crackle of cherrywood, the heavy metal scrape of iron lids that covered the firebox. Bessie Gunter's cookbook is like that old cookstove, designed to get things done with a minimum of pretense and bother. May Gunter, a relative of the cookbook compiler, contributed a narrative on how "To Pick Up Terrapin":

> *Before cooking a terrapin allow it to swim about for three or four hours in cold water to cleanse it. Then wash it off and take it out and plunge it head first into a pot of boiling water. This will kill it instantly. Cover the pot up tight. Boil until feet skin easily. Then take off the feet, removing from them the skin and toe nails. Take off the under shell and take away from it any meat that may cling to it. Remove the head and tail and carefully take the gall from the liver and any portion of the liver which looks greenish. It is best to cut off all the liver possible and then remove the gall. Do not pull or squeeze it or it will surely break. Remove the sand bag, which is a brown spongy substance which lies under the top shell on either side of the ridge and can easily be distinguished. Pour all the remaining contents of the upper shell into the stew pan and stew with butter, milk, and cream and season with salt and pepper, if desired. Some use wine, I do not.*

Miss Corson, another contributor, suggested a cream sauce for the terrapin:

> *Take a tablespoonful of butter and one of flour and put them into a saucepan over the fire until they bubble. Keep stirring until they are smoothly mixed, then begin to add cream or rich milk, stirring all the time. To one pint of terrapin meat, liver, and juice, you allow one pint of cream. Season with salt, a little cayenne pepper, and grated nutmeg, and then add terrapin meat. After the terrapin becomes scalding hot in the sauce, and just before it is ready to serve, add the yolks of four raw eggs, beaten up a little, one gill of Madeira wine, a tablespoon of lemon juice, and serve.*

Now we're cooking. In Bessie Gunter's day, plunging a live terrapin headfirst into a pot of boiling water was not considered an act of animal cruelty. That was how you cooked terrapins. Most of the contributors to her cookbook were rural people who lived close to the earth and to the water around them. They killed hogs in the late fall and put the carcasses into a tub of boiling water to loosen the hair, which they scraped off with a clam shell. Then they hung the hogs from gallows made of oak. They slit them open, took out the organ meat and then cut them up and put the hams and chops in the smokehouse to cure. They ground up the sidemeat, cleaned out the intestines and then stuffed the intestines with sidemeat to make sausage. They used every part of the hog, wasted nothing, even made soap by adding lye to the fat.

The methods of preparing terrapin tend to be simple in the rural south of Delmarva. All that is needed is a high-quality terrapin—a count—and other than that perhaps some butter and salt and pepper. Black coffee and whiskey and biscuits are the spartan sides. As you travel north, you begin to see butter and cream, rich milk, egg yolks and various liquors. In Maryland, terrapin soup recipes sometimes included onion, celery and herbs such as thyme, parsley and marjoram. Jane Howard, in *Fifty Years in a Maryland Kitchen*, suggested this procedure:

> *The terrapin must be alive. Drop it into boiling water and let it stay there five minutes. Remove it, rub the skin off the feet, tail, and head, drawing the latter out with a skewer. Put the terrapin again in boiling water and cook for fifteen to thirty minutes, till tender, depending on the size and age. Test by pressing the feet. Let it cool in the water. Then remove it, draw the nails from the feet, cut off the under shell, lift off the upper shell. Remove carefully the gall bladder and throw it away, sand bags, heart, and intestines. Leave liver and eggs.*
>
> *Separate it at the joints and cut meat into pieces about one inch long. Put the meat, liver, and eggs in a saucepan with two quarts of boiling water and cook with seasonings until the meat falls from the bones. The pot should be covered loosely, and cooked slowly.*

Mrs. Howard then added to the soup two sliced onions, three celery stalks finely chopped, the juice of one lemon and one-quarter cup sherry or Madeira, along with a teaspoon each of chopped thyme, parsley, allspice and marjoram, plus a little mace.

"Skim the soup while it boils," she advised. "Strain it when ready to serve, reheat, and for each quart of soup have ready one yolk of a hard-cooked egg rubbed smooth with a little butter and flour. Place a tablespoon of Sherry or Madeira in each hot soup plate, stir the egg yolk mixture into the steaming soup, stir and serve."

Sometimes a terrapin will have eggs, sometimes not. Howard had a little trick to create her own eggs in case the terrapin was without. She mixed four hard-cooked chicken egg yolks with one uncooked yolk to make a paste. Then she shaped the paste into round balls the size of marbles. These were dropped into boiling water, cooked for two minutes and then added to the terrapin soup as a garnish.

And now we have nearly completed the circle of the diamondback terrapin's journey through our gustatory folklife. Terrapins fed hungry soldiers during the Revolution. They were fed to slaves in such quantities the slaves protested. They became central to social gatherings in the rural farmland of Delmarva, and then they went on to star in the greatest restaurants in our great cities. The final click to complete our circle takes us off the Delmarva Peninsula to Baltimore, where terrapins became the darling of politicians, wealthy businessmen and socialites.

In 1932, Frederick Philip Steiff compiled an anthology of recipes (he called them receipts) titled *Eat, Drink and Be Merry in Maryland*. In it, he relates the annual gatherings of the Lobby Club, founded in 1888 by Commodore Thornton Rollins of Baltimore. The club met once a year at the home of Commodore Rollins for a terrapin banquet. "Probably no terrapin served in Baltimore was wider heralded than this," wrote Steiff. "The banquet was a natural sequence to a convivial stag party at the theatre. The membership was composed only of the contemporary bon-vivants de luxe, epicures, and gourmets. Naught but terrapin and champagne has ever been served. Today Commodore Rollins is a figure loved, respected, and honored by all who revere the fine art of living as practiced during the last century in Baltimore."

When it comes to putting on a bacchanalian carousal, Baltimore gets it.

Chapter 4

MUSKRAT MUSKRAT CANDLELIGHT

When my wife, Lynn, and I celebrated our thirty-fifth wedding anniversary a few years ago, we decided to do something different. In the past, we had taken nice trips, eaten at fancy restaurants and one year spent the weekend at Captain Buddy Harrison's Chesapeake House on Tilghman Island fishing for rock and eating oysters. For our thirty-fifth, we decided to have a muskrat dinner.

Muskrats are popular in some parts of Delmarva but not others. I grew up in the far south of Delmarva in Virginia, and most folks I knew didn't eat muskrat. They trapped them and sold the pelts, but I don't recall anyone eating them. When I told some friends we were going to eat muskrats for our anniversary, they discreetly asked if anything was wrong. If you need to borrow a few bucks, just let me know.

Muskrat dinners seem to be a Maryland tradition. Churches have them, and popular neighborhood restaurants will often have "muskrat nights" during the winter season. Muskrats are especially popular in Dorchester County, which is not surprising considering the landscape. Cambridge is the county seat and is a bustling town with a deep-water port on the Choptank River, a historic waterway where a skipjack fleet numbering in the hundreds once dredged oysters under sail.

But if you leave Cambridge and head south and west, you will find a vast landscape of bay country wetlands, a place where the term *sea level* is ever apparent and at times ominous. This is a land of open spaces interrupted now and then by forested hummocks, a place where two-lane roads wind through marshes that seem on the same plane as the roadway. Now and then you'll see grassy mounds scattered here and there across the marsh. These would be the dens of muskrats, fur-bearing relatives of beavers that have been trapped in this rural area for generations.

It is indeed a unique landscape, especially in the southern part of the county where Lakesville Road winds its way from Golden Hill through Crapo, Wingate, Bishops Head and, finally, Crocheron, where it comes to an uncelebrated end at Hooper Strait. This is called the Straits District, and it is about thirty-five miles from Cambridge, but it is in a different world. Here, the workboats outnumber the pleasure boats, and Chesapeake Bay deadrises are as common here as yachts are in St. Michaels. People here still make a living working on the water, and that still means trapping muskrats.

Before the invention of modern lightweight insulating fabrics now prevalent in outdoor wear, muskrat furs meant big money in this part of Dorchester County. Most were exported to European countries for use in coats and other garments, and trapping was just as important to a waterman's income as oystering and crabbing. The pelts were sent to market, and the muskrats were roasted for the family dinner or sold in the market.

Muskrats no longer generate a lot of income, but the tradition lives on. Dorchester's National Outdoor Show each February is all about muskrats, including competitions for skinning and cooking them. The Outdoor Show has been around since 1938, and it draws visitors from all over the country, including the big bald guy who hosts *Bizarre Foods with Andrew Zimmern*.

People in Dorchester County obviously know something the rest of us don't. We were determined to see what all the fuss was about muskrats, and the thirty-fifth anniversary seemed as good a time as any to try. We hunt and fish. We like wild game. So, we went to see our friend Susan Fletcher, who runs Susan's Seafood in the town of New Church, Virginia. Susan sells flounder and oysters and crabs like every seafood dealer should, but she also sells muskrats when they are in season in winter.

Mike Walker, a local trapper, keeps her supplied, and she has found that muskrats still are very popular among local people who might have had them growing up. A few years ago, she would sell 1,000 rats during the season, which runs from December 1 through the end of February. Pelts would go to buyers in Russia who paid $8 or more for each, and the animal would be sold at the seafood store. Pelts bring about $1.75 these days, and the muskrats sell for around $5 each, depending on size. In 2020, Susan sold 651 of Mike's muskrats, down a bit from previous years. "We had a lot of flooding, and Mike couldn't get his traps set," Susan explains.

The market for muskrats is mixed about evenly by race, Susan said. "Basically, if your family ate muskrats when you were growing up, you're still likely to want them today. There are not many new converts to muskrats."

We picked out two large, fresh ones, and Susan put them in a plastic bag and iced them down. When I was growing up, our family had a motto: if it dies, it fries. That means, if you go gunning and kill something, you bring it home and eat it. When I started duck hunting, I didn't bring home many black ducks and mallards, but I did bring home numerous buffleheads and hooded mergansers. These are fish-eating ducks, and some people don't like them because they "taste fishy." I've always liked the taste of fish, so I didn't have a problem with that. I decided that the perfect way to cook our muskrats would be similar to the way I prepared hooded mergansers.

I removed the four legs, keeping as much meat as possible, and then removed the saddle in one piece, cutting the backbone in front of and behind the meaty section. I discarded the ribs and the part of the backbone not attached to the saddle. As I did with the duck, I soaked the parts for twenty-four hours, refrigerated, in salted water, to which I added a quartered onion, about a quarter cup of vinegar and a squeeze of Sriracha hot sauce.

I dried the marinated parts with a paper towel and seasoned them with salt and pepper, placed them in a single layer in a roasting pan and then added an orange glaze consisting of a mixture of orange juice, some hardy pinot noir and orange marmalade. I roasted the muskrats for about an hour at 300 degrees Fahrenheit, keeping them covered with foil for the first thirty to forty-five minutes, and then removed the foil to let the sauce thicken. While the muskrats were cooking, I baked sweet potatoes and cooked wild rice and turnip greens seasoned with fatback. Our anniversary dinner was almost ready.

A little candlelight, some appropriate music and a glass of the pinot noir, and here we have orange-glazed muskrat with sweet potato, wild rice and turnip greens. The flavor was assertive, wild but tamed by the sweet orange sauce, a nice foil for the sweetness of the potato and turnip greens—reminiscent, perhaps, of hooded merganser.

Chapter 5

OF ROBIN SNIPE AND CALICO BACKS

The Delmarva Peninsula is a vital part of the East Coast migration corridor used by many species of birds. In the fall, great flocks of waterfowl come down from their nesting grounds in the north. Some pass through on their way to warmer regions south of us, but if the weather is mild, many will stay right here in the seaside bays and marshes and the creeks and rivers of the Chesapeake Bay.

In spring, tens of thousands of shorebirds move through. Some, such as the red knot, will rest here for a few days, replenish their fat reserves with the eggs of horseshoe crabs, and then continue north to the prairie provinces of Canada to nest. Sandpipers and dunlin follow the same pattern, pausing to rest and refuel before heading north to the tundra.

Some shorebirds stay here all summer, nesting on the barrier islands and remote marshes. Piping plovers nest on shell-littered washovers, their eggs almost invisible among the spent shells. Black skimmers, American oystercatchers and willets build shallow nests not far above the high waterline. Clapper rails build well-hidden nests in the spartina grasses, often heard but seldom seen during the summer.

Gulls and terns are likewise dependent on coastal marshes. Usually around mid-March, laughing gulls show up and will nest in the high marsh. Ring-billed gulls, after spending the winter with us, will move north. Forster's terns, least terns and the much larger Caspian and royal terns nest on scrapes on the barrier islands, often among colonies of skimmers and oystercatchers.

Above: A black-bellied plover in breeding plumage. This bird would have been fair game before laws were passed in 1918.

Left: A flock of dunlin at Blackwater National Wildlife Refuge near Cambridge, Maryland.

All of these birds, in one way or another, have played a role in the native food culture of Delmarva. Until the birds were protected by federal law, they were legal game. Spring shorebird shooting attracted sportsmen from all over the country, who came to the barrier island gunning clubs and hotels during the spring migration to shoot red knots, dunlin, sandpipers, willets and whimbrels, which were called Hudsonian curlew.

Local people took advantage of the nesting birds to collect the eggs of gulls and clapper rails. Some eggs would be taken for home use, but many would be sold at markets along with other game and fish. Place names on Delmarva still reflect this custom. Egging Marsh is on the map, just a few miles east of the village of Quinby. It's a vast plain of spartina grass, firm

American oystercatchers nest on the barrier island beaches. Their populations were decimated during the era of shorebird shooting.

underfoot and perfect for colonies of nesting laughing gulls and rails, which were known as marsh hens or sedge hens.

The assault on migrating and nesting shorebirds, gulls and terns didn't begin and end with the kitchen in mind. In the late 1800s and early 1900s, bird feathers were all the rage in the millinery trade. A fashionable woman's Easter bonnet might include the plumes of snowy egrets, or perhaps the silky white feathers of the least tern. Egrets and terns were not shot for the table but for fashion.

Spring shorebird shooting created linguistics all its own. Birds were named creatively and descriptively. The red knot, for example, was called the robin snipe because it had a red breast and belly when it was in its spring breeding plumage. Likewise, the ruddy turnstone, normally a drab gray bird, was called the calico back because of the colorful pattern it wore during mating season. Curiously, willets were called gray backs, which is surprising because during spring migration the willets have a handsome mottled plumage. Terns were called strikers because of their practice of hovering over water and then suddenly dropping down with a splash to catch a fish. Great blue herons were called crankies because of the grating call they made in flight. Ospreys were fish hawks, kestrels were sparrow hawks and immature bald eagles were gray eagles.

There is surprisingly little mention of shorebirds and wild game eggs in the cookbooks of the day. When Bessie Gunter's cookbook came out in 1889, spring shorebird shooting was at its peak. She tells us how to cook partridge or bobwhite quail, but there is no mention of robin snipe, calico backs or Hudsonian curlew. Jane Howard covers duck, partridge and pheasant in her *Fifty Years in a Maryland Kitchen* but nary a marsh hen. In Steiff's *Eat, Drink and Be Merry in Maryland*, canvasback duck, frog legs, rabbit and bear made the cut, but the gray back did not.

In reading the accounts of spring shorebird shooting by writers of the period such as Alexander Hunter, it is apparent birds were killed by the hundreds in a single hunt, yet there is scant mention of what happened to the birds *après la chasse*. Shorebird shooting was done during warm months, and there was little refrigeration available on the beaches and marshes where they were hunted. One must suspect that many of the birds were wasted.

The combination of spring shooting, egging and supplying the millinery industry took its toll, and in 1916 and 1918, federal laws were passed to

The ruddy turnstone in breeding plumage was called a "calico back."

Sandpipers are small shorebirds found on the beaches and tidal flats. This one is a least sandpiper.

protect birds during the spring nesting season. A man who played a major role in protecting the birds was a former congressman, pioneering wildlife photographer and contributor to *National Geographic* magazine. His name was George Shiras.

George Shiras: With Camera and Flashlight

Many of us grew up vicariously exploring the universe through the colorful images of *National Geographic* magazine. For well over a century, *National Geographic* has set the standard for excellence in photography, writing and interpreting the world around us. But *National Geographic* was not always a photographic magazine. It is published by the National Geographic Society, which was formed by thirty-three founding members on January 13, 1888, in Washington, D.C. The purpose was to create a "society for the increase

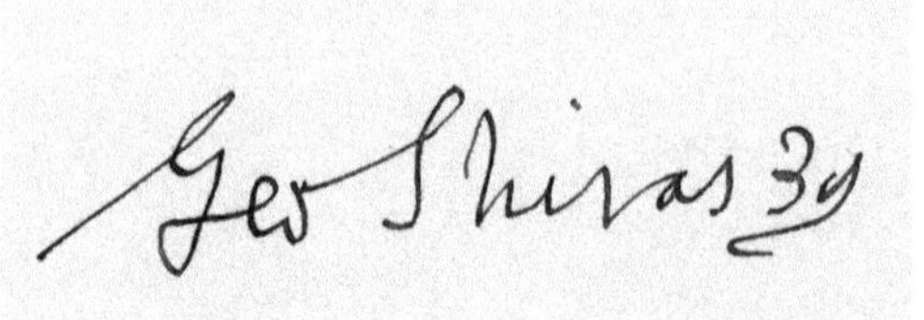

George Shiras signed his name "3d."

and diffusion of geographic knowledge." The society published its first magazine in October 1888, and it was sent to two hundred members of the scientific community.

So, the colorful magazine that has taken us everywhere from the depths of the ocean to the vastness of space was born a professional journal, boasting a pedigree more closely aligned with academia than family entertainment.

That changed because of a relationship between Gilbert H. Grosvenor, who became editor of the magazine in 1903, and George Shiras III, a Pittsburgh lawyer whose father was a Supreme Court justice. Shiras (who signed his name "Shiras 3d") was himself a lawyer and politician, having served in the U.S. Congress, but he also enjoyed hunting and fishing and was a keen naturalist. In Congress, he helped lay the foundation for legislation that later would become the Migratory Bird Law of 1916 and the Migratory Bird Treaty Act of 1918.

In 1889, at age thirty, Shiras purchased his first camera and began taking it in the field, using some of the same skills and techniques he had used in hunting to capture wildlife on film. He quickly became obsessed with capturing wild animals and birds in their natural environment. He often photographed at night, stalking animals with a kerosene lantern and using magnesium flash to freeze action. He used trip lines attached to the camera to make his quarry take a "selfie," and he used blinds, decoys, sneak boats, jacklights and other hunting tools and techniques he had employed as a young man, hunting mainly in the Lake Superior area of Michigan, where his family had a vacation home.

Shiras was a prolific photographer, and his family had sufficient resources that he could afford to spend a great deal of time in the field stalking wild game with his camera. By the early 1900s, he had assembled an impressive portfolio of photographs, many of which were taken at night.

In 1905, while serving in Congress, Shiras visited Gilbert Grosvenor at the National Geographic Society office in Washington and showed him a portfolio of prints. Grosvenor was immediately taken by the stark beauty and drama of the photographs and told Shiras he wanted to publish them. Grosvenor had just published the magazine's first photographs—eleven images taken in Tibet—but after seeing Shiras's work, Grosvenor decided to devote an entire issue of the magazine to his photographs.

Seventy-four of Shiras's photographs appeared in the July 1906 issue, with very little text, and the reaction was swift and varied. The public loved the issue, which the magazine had to reprint to meet demand, and membership in the society swelled. The society's board, however, was not so enamored. Some felt that publishing a journal filled with photographs did not reflect the society's high-minded mission of "diffusing geographic knowledge." Two members of the board resigned in disgust, objecting that their journal had been relegated to a "picture book."

Grosvenor feared for his job, but apparently the flood of membership checks convinced his bosses that there was a future in publishing wildlife photography. Grosvenor and Shiras worked together many more times. Shiras was elected to the society's board in 1911, and in 1935, *National Geographic* published Shiras's two-volume classic, *Hunting Wild Life with Camera and Flashlight.*

Although Shiras was from Pennsylvania, much of his photographic work was centered on the Marquette area of Michigan, where his family spent their summers. As a young man, he learned to hunt and fish, often going out with Native American guides. Shiras also had a strong Delmarva tie. In 1894, he joined the Revels Island Shooting Club, an association of wealthy northern businessmen who owned several thousand acres along the coast of the Eastern Shore near Wachapreague, Virginia. The property included a large clubhouse, where members would gather to socialize, and it also had several cottages owned by individual members. Shiras built a large two-story frame dwelling with a wide front porch and stone fireplaces. The home also included a photographic darkroom, where Shiras would develop the photos taken on his daily outings.

Hunting Wild Life with Camera and Flashlight includes two chapters on Shiras's Revels Island days, along with forty-two photographs taken on the island. These chapters provide important documentation of what life was like in the hunting clubs that proliferated along the coast in the late 1800s and early 1900s and are now gone. Periodicals of the day frequently included articles about visits to gunning clubs and island hotels, and these can be found in various online archives today. But here we have an account written by a club member, documented with his own photographs, which were developed in a darkroom in his island home.

The NATIONAL GEOGRAPHIC MAGAZINE

Vol. XVII JULY, 1906 No. 7

CONTENTS

"Photographing Wild Game with Flash-light and Camera"

By Hon. GEORGE SHIRAS, Third
Member of Congress 1903-1905

With a Series of 70 Illustrations of Wild Game—Deer, Elk, Bull Moose, Raccoon, Porcupine, Wild Cat, Herons, Ducks, Snowy Owl, Pelicans, Birds in Flight, etc.

Published by the National Geographic Society
Hubbard Memorial Hall
Washington, D. C.

$2.50 a Year 25 Cents a Number

Entered at the Post-Office in Washington, D. C., as Second-Class Mail Matter

George Shiras was the first photographer to have an exclusive showing in the pages of *National Geographic*. This is the July 1906 issue.

Shiras was a part-time resident of Revels Island for nearly forty years, and his accounts in *Hunting Wild Life* reflect his strong commitment to conservation as well as his growing interest in photography. Shiras was only twenty-five when he began spending time on Revels Island, but he was concerned then that practices such as spring shorebird shooting were not sustainable and would eventually prove harmful to wildlife. Shiras noticed in his early days on the island that shorebird numbers already were dwindling.

"It is not strange that eventually a tremendous decrease in shorebirds was observed during migrations," he wrote, "for in the spring when the local shorebirds were either nesting or mating, every clubhouse from Virginia to New Jersey was filled with members intent on hunting shorebirds at a season when all other shooting was prohibited."

Shiras described shorebird shooting as wholesale slaughter and a wasteful practice. "Day after day, I have seen otherwise reputable sportsmen bring in 200 birds, and when the weather was warm it was practically impossible to keep such birds from spoiling," he wrote.

Shiras took up photography during his early years at the club and began hunting shorebirds with the camera. The result is a remarkable collection of photographs of yellowlegs, red knots, pectoral sandpipers, ruddy turnstones and other shorebirds coming in to decoys handmade by local artisans.

In addition to being a lawyer and photographer, Shiras was a politician who served in the Pennsylvania state legislature and was elected to the United States Congress in 1903. He served for only one term and declined a nomination for reelection, but during his two years in office, Shiras helped lay the groundwork for conservation legislation that would protect migrating birds.

Shiras was especially concerned about the red knot, or robin snipe. While a member of Congress, Shiras went to Revels Island to document the bird, whose population was dwindling. "Late in May 1904 I made a special trip to Revels Island to obtain pictures of what I feared might be a doomed species," Shiras wrote.

Shiras set up a rig of wooden decoys in front of a blind near the water's edge and spent the afternoon photographing the birds. "I obtained a fine series of pictures of the entire flock as its members circled back time after time to satisfy their innocent curiosity concerning the strange wooden counterfeits," he wrote.

Shiras's final visit to Revels Island came in May 1923, when he was accompanied by Dr. E.W. Nelson, chief of the U.S. Biological Survey. The visit, wrote Shiras, was to assess the effectiveness of the migratory bird laws passed in 1916 and 1918. "The launch had no sooner put out from the little port town of Wachapreague, than Hudsonian curlews (whimbrels) began springing up on all sides and we observed nearly a thousand on the six-mile trip. Yet, this bird had nearly become extinct ten years before," wrote Shiras.

Shiras and Nelson spent several days exploring the salt marshes and tidal flats of Revels Island and discovered that the populations of knots, willets, dunlins, plovers, dowitchers, turnstones and sandpipers had indeed responded well to the conservation laws. The lone exception was the yellowlegs, which Shiras said could still be legally hunted. Additional legislation was passed in 1927 closing the season on yellowlegs.

In his lifetime, George Shiras III accomplished three significant firsts. He became America's first real wildlife photographer, putting together an amazing collection of action pictures of birds and mammals going about their daily and nightly business. He recognized the folly of allowing shorebirds to be killed as they were mating and nesting, and he was among the first to persuade Congress to outlaw the practice. And, last but not least, he was the first to have a cover-to-cover photo spread in *National Geographic*. Were it not for Shiras, *National Geographic* might today still be a boring academic journal.

In 1928, George Shiras donated 2,400 glass plate negatives to the National Geographic Society, and today the archive is still intact. Most of the photographs were taken in the Lake Superior area of Michigan, and most of the images were taken of animals at night. The photographs of Revels Island are something of a departure in that they were taken during the daytime, but still they make use of some of the tools of the hunt, such as decoys, to lure birds into camera range. And they were revolutionary in that they captured birds in flight.

An exhibition of Shiras's work was shown in 2016 at the Musée de la Chasse et de la Nature in Paris, and the prints for this were made from scans of Shiras's original glass plates. A companion book—*George Shiras: In the Heart of the Dark Night*—includes many of the photographs in the exhibit. It was written by Jean-Christophe Bailly and edited by Sonia Voss, who also was curator of the exhibition.

The Shiras book associated with the Paris exhibition is available via the usual retail booksellers, and the two-volume set *Hunting Wild Life with Camera and Flashlight* turns up now and then in used bookstores.

Shiras would likely be amused to find that his photographs were being shown in a museum in Paris and are now considered works of art. Shiras was a lawyer, politician and photographer, but mostly he was a naturalist and conservationist. To him, photography was part of the process of documenting the lives of birds and animals. On Revels Island, for example, he photographed bird nests and bird eggs in a manner that could be described as obsessive. In Yellowstone National Park, he discovered a subspecies of moose, which was named for him.

Shiras also turns up in Ernest Hemingway's short story "Homage to Switzerland" as two men discuss *National Geographic* magazine. The dialogue goes like this:

"I enjoyed, too, the wild animal photographs of George Shiras three."

"They were damned fine."

"I beg your pardon."

"They were excellent. That fellow Shiras?"

"You call him fellow?"

"We're old friends," said Harris.

"I see. You know George Shiras three? He must be very interesting."

"He is. He's about the most interesting man I know."

Bailey's Birds

Harold H. Bailey published a book titled *The Birds of Virginia* in 1913, at the height of the popularity of spring shorebird shooting. His description of coastal species provides a chilling narrative as to the toll that was being taken by spring gunners, as well as by those in the millinery trade. Here are a few samples:

> *Willet—This was formerly a very abundant game bird all along our coast, often being found in numbers even on the lower shores of our large rivers and the Chesapeake Bay. It is, however, fast becoming a bird of the past, and within a few years they will be considered a rare bird with our coast sportsmen. Being one of the earliest birds to lay, many are shot by the spring gunners after being mated and with eggs, a condition sure to diminish if not exterminate any species of bird no matter how plentiful.*
>
> *Least Tern (aka, Little Striker, Sea Swallow)—Formerly one of the most abundant of sea birds, this beautiful little tern is now almost extinct as a breeding bird on our coast. A few pairs do, however, breed near the southern boundary line, and north of us. In 1889 these birds were so numerous that a large colony were breeding on the mainland beach, at the entrance of Back River into the Chesapeake Bay. Shortly after this, the slaughter commenced;*

the birds being shot and skinned for the millinery trade of the large northern cities. During the breeding season on the islands, sometimes three to five hundred birds were shot in a single day. This slaughter went on for a few seasons, the number of birds diminishing each year until they disappeared from our shores almost entirely, and the market gunners could not further make a living shooting and skinning these birds at ten cents each, the price paid by the wholesale millinery houses.

Black Skimmer (Flood Gull, Cut-water)—Of all the sea birds nesting on our coast, this species is holding its own and increasing more rapidly than any other species. The apparent reason for this is that they arrive from the south late in the spring, about May 5th, when all the gunning after beach birds is practically finished, and therefore is seldom shot by the gunners for sport.

Caspian Tern (Gannet Striker)—Like the least tern, this handsome large tern is now a rare bird in our territory, although a few pair still breed on one of our coastal islands. It was never thought as common a bird as the royal tern. The changed conditions of the islands affecting their breeding grounds has had much to do with their leaving our territory for nesting sites elsewhere.

Snowy Egret—It formerly was quite an abundant breeder, but like other species noted, it gave way before the demand for millinery purposes, until now they are one of our rarest birds. These are the birds most noted for their feathers worn on women's hats, the demand for which nearly exterminated them.

Piping Plover (Little Plover, Ring-neck)—This is another bird fast becoming extinct on our coast, the main reason for which is that they are shot at by the gunners who are after spring beach birds, when other larger varieties are lacking. They are tame little fellows, and when driven to curiosity will come within a few feet of a person sitting still on the sand dunes.

American Oystercatcher (Sea Crow)—This is the next bird to become extinct on our Virginia coast, for it is truly a scarce bird now. Formerly it was fairly plentiful all along the coastal and inland sandy beaches, but of late years it has become so scarce that none of our islands can boast of over one or two pair of breeding birds, some not that.

SECTION III

We Plow, We Propagate

Chapter 1

GROWING OUR OWN

Self-sufficiency has always been a tradition on rural Delmarva. Most of us are only two or three generations separated from a time when we ate what we grew on the farm and in the garden or what we hunted and gathered in the nearby woods, fields, creeks and bays. Even today, when we live in the shadow of a Walmart or Food Lion, we still plant our gardens. Seeds are ordered in February, and onions, peas, lettuce, chard, kale and pak choi go in as soon as the ground can be worked in March. By then, the seed potatoes are ready, the little eyes beginning to dimple and grow. The potato is sliced so that there are two or three eyes on each piece, and it goes into the ground, eyes up, and is covered with soil.

After the last frost date—April 15 where we live—the tomatoes are planted beneath a trellis. The lower leaves are pinched off, and the plant goes in deep. We hoard coffee cups from McDonald's over the winter, and we slice off the bottoms and place the cup over the plant to serve as a collar. The collar protects the tender plant and prevents cutworms from killing it. We plant Better Boys and similar varieties for canning and freezing, and we splurge and put in some heirlooms—Cherokee Purple and Mr. Stripey—that will go on a BLT sometime shortly after July 4, our target date for vine-ripened tomatoes.

We'll also plant tomatillos, little green gems wrapped with a tissue-like husk. These will go raw in a salad or perhaps smoked on the grill and made into a salsa. We also plant peppers, a hot variety called Long Red Slim. These will be harvested in September or October after they turn red, the

This garden has tomatoes for freezing and canning, but the heirlooms are for bacon, lettuce and tomato sandwiches in July and August.

stems removed, and they will be packed into bottles with vinegar, sugar and salt. The spicy vinegar is a perfect accent for collard greens or coleslaw.

By late June, we'll be grabbling potatoes, gently scraping around the plant to find a few large enough to eat, to have with a fresh crab cake and some new peas from the garden. In two more weeks, all the potatoes will be dug, rubbed gently and put away in a dark place until needed. A freshly dug potato is unlike anything that comes from a store. The peel is not so much a covering but simply a layer of color. You can peel a redskin potato by rubbing it with your thumb. But then, why would you want to do that? We rinse them, boil them in a little salted water and in a few minutes have them with butter and chives.

We find a sense of self-sufficiency in growing our own vegetables, and there is comfort in knowing where they came from. That rarely happens in a grocery store.

Gardening is a central part of Delmarva's food culture, and it reflects our agrarian past. Gardens today do not resemble farms, which after World War II became larger and more mechanized, specializing in grain crops to support our robust poultry industry. A few generations ago, a farm more closely resembled what we consider a garden today. My great-grandparents

These redskin potatoes will be going from garden to table in just minutes. That's the reward of growing your own.

farmed. They planted about sixty acres and raised seven kids, most of whom went to college. Two of those children became farmers, and one taught agriculture. My father wanted a job where he could wear a tie to work. He got a degree in accounting and went to work for the Eastern Shore of Virginia Produce Exchange.

Written accounts of my great-grandparents' farm depict a land of great diversity. They grew vegetables and potatoes for market, but there also were a variety of fruit trees and grape arbors for making wine. They grew figs and made preserves when the fruit ripened in August, and they saved the rind from their watermelons and made pickles from it. They had chickens and ducks, hogs and a few head of cattle. They lived on a seaside creek, where fish, clams and crabs could be taken in summer and where oysters grew fat for winter harvest. They fed themselves with what they grew or gathered, and they sold enough to buy things like coffee and sugar and other necessities.

Looking back, I realize my father was the first man in my family to hold a regular job.

Hog Killing

Most farm families killed hogs in the winter, usually between Thanksgiving and Christmas. Hog killing was not exclusively a Delmarva tradition—rural people all over the country did it—but it was an important part of life here until, like the rest of America, we started buying sausage made by a Chinese company and named for a dead country music star.

Hog killing on Delmarva was often a family affair. Families tended to be larger several generations ago, and when families grew, they settled not far from the main branch. My grandparents had a farm, and when their sons went out on their own, they bought farms not far from my grandparents. When it came time to kill hogs, all would gather at my grandparents' place for a few days of ritual and hard work that initiated the winter season.

An old Winchester Model 1890 .22-caliber rifle hangs on the wall in our family room, and visitors probably wonder why we feel it necessary to have a gun openly displayed. The old .22 is pump-operated and has an octagonal barrel. It is a classic. It also is the rifle my grandfather used to dispatch hogs during hog killing. It is the rifle my father used to teach me how to responsibly handle a dangerous weapon.

We visited my grandparents most Sunday afternoons, and if the weather was good, we'd take out the old .22 and walk down the field road, past the hog pen and down to the woods edge. There, we would shoot a few tin cans or anything else we could find that would make a good target.

If anyone asks about the old Winchester, I just tell them it's my link with the past. It makes me think about country ham and sausage.

Our family's last hog killing took place after my grandparents had passed on, so it was just my two uncles and their families and a few friends. My uncles contracted with some local men to do most of the work. They traveled around the community at hog-killing time, stopping in at farms to offer their services, much as a midwife might assist at childbirth. Years ago, families would have killed a half dozen or more hogs to supply multiple families with winter meat, but we would kill only three.

The men were experienced in the old ways. They began by building fires under two large tubs filled with water, and then they went into the woods and cut several armloads of pine boughs and put them in the water. While the water was heating, the men killed the hogs, one man shooting the hog between the eyes, another slitting the animal's throat to let it quickly bleed to death.

Above: The hogs are hung and butchered.

Left: Water is heated in metal barrels and then scooped out to fill tubs, into which the hogs are placed.

A metal scraper is used to shave the hair from the body of the hog.

When the hogs were dead, they were placed in the tubs of boiling water, and the men used metal tools to scrape the hair from their bodies. Years ago, large clam shells were used for this purpose. The hogs were then removed from the tubs and hung by their hind legs from tripods made from pine trees about ten feet in length.

The men then began the process of dismantling the hogs. Intestines were removed and placed in aluminum basins. These would be cleaned thoroughly, and the small intestines would be used to make sausage. The large intestine would be used to make chitterlings.

The hams, shoulders, ribs and chops were removed, and the organ meats were cooked with seasonings and cornmeal and chopped to make scrapple. The fat was placed in a black kettle over a fire and was slowly rendered down, with someone constantly stirring. When it was done, it was placed in a press and the lard was squeezed out and saved for cooking.

The feet and head were thoroughly cleaned and cooked. The feet and ears would be soaked for several days, then chopped up and seasoned with vinegar and spices to make souse. Other parts of the head such as the jowls would be preserved with salt and later used as seasoning in cooking. My

The fat from the hog is boiled down to make lard, which is used in cooking.

grandmother highly valued the jowl for cooking, pronouncing it "hog's jole," giving it a nice repetition of the *o* sound.

Many years later Lynn and I were in Washington, D.C., for some sightseeing. The hotel where we stayed had a French restaurant that was highly regarded, so we decided to have dinner there. The salad they served, in addition to the usual greens, included *lardons*, which were not familiar to me. I wasn't familiar with the term, but I instantly recognized what I was eating. It was Grandma's "hog's jole."

Chapter 2
TO MARKET, TO MARKET

The prevalent notion these days is that before the opening of the Chesapeake Bay Bridge in 1952 and the Chesapeake Bay Bridge-Tunnel in 1964, our peninsula was a remote, rural, wild and somewhat backward land where people clung to old ways and pushed back against the enlightenment of modern times.

True, perhaps, but you have to realize that this thought is based on a framework of roads, bridges and motor vehicles. When the highway era began, water became a barrier. It isolated us. But prior to the highways and bridges, water was our means of travel; it joined us with cities north and south, it connected us with foreign countries, foreign cultures. Water was our highway; it is how we traveled and how we got the food we grew and gathered to market.

It is true that the peninsula was rural, as was most of America in those days, but the Eastern Shore was no more remote than any other region. In fact, with our infrastructure of bays, rivers, creeks and ocean inlets, we had a transportation system that easily connected us with one another and with the world beyond.

My great-grandfather John had a farm on Red Bank Creek in Northampton County, Virginia. He also had a schooner that he used to ship goods to northern cities and to sail to the West Indies for cargo that varied from sugar and spices to bird guano used for fertilizer. Being a farmer, John never threw anything away, and after his death, our family found letters, receipts and other papers that indicate that, although he lived in a rural area, he was very much connected with the rest of the world.

In 1848, word spread that James Marshall had discovered gold near Sutter's Fort in California. John and his older brother, Thomas, decided to join the tens of thousands who took off to seek fortune and adventure in the gold fields of the West. Some traveled across the country, and others came by boat. Thomas and John were both experienced sailors, so they chose the latter method of travel. They left their home port of Red Bank and sailed north to New York. On March 3, 1849, they boarded the schooner *James L. Day* and left for California. Thomas had recently celebrated his nineteenth birthday. John was fifteen.

The brothers sailed from New York around Cape Horn and then took a northern route up the coast. It was a long trip, made even longer by currents and prevailing winds that forced ships to make a wide swing nearly to the longitude of the Hawaiian Islands. This would be the last journey of this distance they would have to endure. One of the many issues raised by the California Gold Rush was the need to efficiently get men and materials to the mining areas in California and to get gold back to banks and mints in the East. A railroad across the swampy isthmus of Panama would shorten the journey by thousands of miles and save weeks of travel time.

The railroad opened in 1850, eliminating the voyage around Cape Horn. The tracks stretched across forty-seven miles of swamp and jungle, linking western Panama City with Aspinwall, a railroad town built on the eastern terminus and named for William H. Aspinwall, the president of the rail company. In 1890, the name was permanently changed to Colon, honoring the explorer Christopher Columbus.

Thomas and John arrived in San Francisco in August 1849, and unfortunately, there are no records to document their adventures during the first months and years of the gold rush. Did they discover gold? Perhaps. Evidence seems to indicate that the brothers thrived in California, especially Thomas. Thomas went into the shipping business with a man named Captain Charles Falkenburg, who appeared to be just as much of an adventurer as he was. The two men owned several ships, and they did business from Mexico to the South China Sea. Did gold finance their shipping business? Or did they simply profit from having a shipping business when commerce was at its peak?

They clearly were successful businessmen. Captain Falkenburg was an expert sailor who set a speed record making the crossing to Manila. He had sailed from Boston to San Francisco via Cape Horn aboard the barquentine *Jane A. Falkenburg*, arriving on New Year's Day 1855. With him was his wife and the namesake of his ship, Jane A. Falkenburg. Captain Falkenburg

Thomas, *left*, and John Badger in the 1850s.

enjoyed the thrill of speed on both land and sea. He and Jane were planning a trip to Sydney, Australia, but before they could leave, Captain Falkenburg was killed while racing his carriage down Telegraph Hill. In a matter of months, his widow and his business partner would be husband and wife.

After Falkenburg's death, Thomas ran the business himself. He bought more ships and expanded his shipping business to include the waters of Australia, Japan, the Sandwich Islands and Mexico. He also operated an amusement park in what is now Oakland.

In old family photographs, Thomas looks like an adventurer. He was a husky, thick-necked, broad-shouldered man with a prominent beard; long, dark hair combed straight back; deep-set, confident eyes; and the body language of a man ready to take on the world. In a family history compiled by my great-aunt Susie Kilham in 1973, he is described as "a blustering, ambitious man, but handicapped by little formal education."

John, on the other hand, looked like a farmer. He was a handsome young man, well dressed, with eyes that were sincere but without fire. He wore an Amish-style beard that covered his chin but no mustache. He would have been a good friend and neighbor, a solid member of his community. He is the man you would want living next door. You would want Thomas manning the helm in the teeth of a gale.

We don't know exactly how long John stayed in California, but we do know that he was back on the farm when war broke out in 1861. Like Thomas, John had a shipping business that he operated out of Red Bank Landing. There is a story in the family that during the war, John was arrested by the Union for running a blockade in the Chesapeake Bay and sent to prison, and his ship was confiscated. Family lore or family fact? The evidence points to the latter. In an 1861 shipping agreement with E.W. Bayly, John agrees to deliver to a buyer in the West Indies 897 bushels of corn and 795 bushels of oats on board the schooner *Louisiana.* That was the last reference made to the *Louisiana.* After the war, John owned a schooner named the *Panama.*

John married Mary Frances Tankard Floyd on November 15, 1865, when he was thirty-three years old and she was twenty-five. They had two sons, Thomas Norman and John Tankard. She was the widow of Richard Floyd and the daughter of J.W.S. and Susan Taylor Tankard. In this letter, written on October 19 and posted in New York, John says he wants to marry Fannie "as soon as I arrive." They were married less than a month later.

> *Dear Fannie,*
>
> *As I promised to write you from this place you will not be surprised at receiving this. You will excuse my delaying it until I am ready for sea. Shall sail for home today. It may be that you will see me before this reaches you. I sincerely hope it may find you all in good health and you may rest assured that you are ever present in my mind. You are the center of all of my future*

hopes. I shall come home prepared to make you my bride and God grant that you may be a happy one. My preparations are not very expensive or extensive. I had rather have your assistance hereafter in purchasing what we may need in setting up our humble household. My fondest hopes are that we may be united as soon as I arrive.
Until then I remain yours most affectionately,
J.W. Badger

In February 1866, John and Fannie made a shopping trip to New York City to furnish their "humble household." They likely took John's schooner *Panama* to New York loaded with freight, unloaded it and then began shopping for household items. Receipts show the purchase of an excelsior mattress

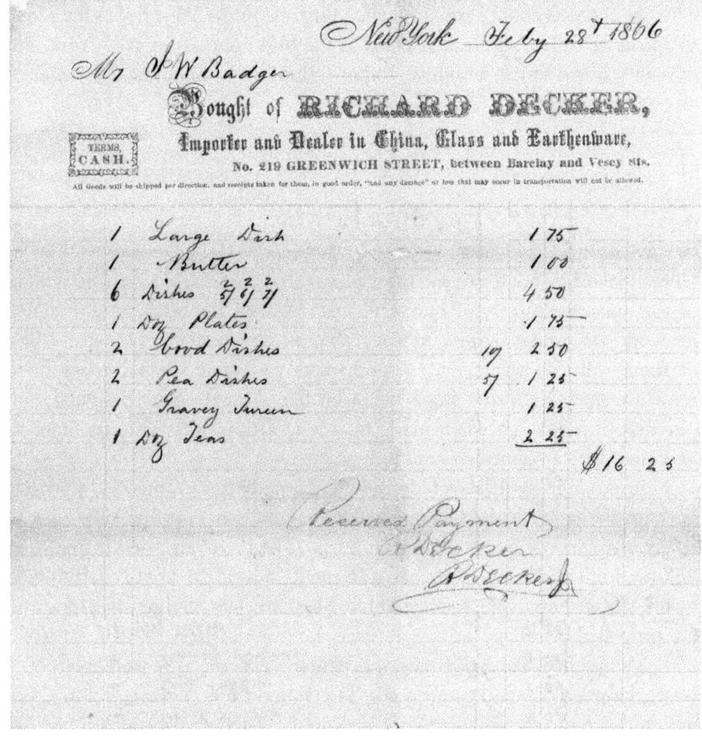

New York Feby 28th 1866

Mr J W Badger

Bought of RICHARD DECKER,

Importer and Dealer in China, Glass and Earthenware,

No. 219 GREENWICH STREET, between Barclay and Vesey Sts.

TERMS, CASH.

All Goods will be shipped per direction, and receipts taken for them, in good order, "and any damage" or loss that may occur in transportation will not be allowed.

1	Large Dish		1 75
1	Butter		1 00
6	Dishes 5/ 6/ 7/		4 50
1	Doz Plates		1 75
2	Covd Dishes	10/	2 50
2	Pea Dishes	5/	1 25
1	Gravey Tureen		1 25
1	Doz Teas		2 25
			$16 25

Received Payment
R Decker
R Decker Jr

The newlyweds stocked up on dinnerware while in New York.

from Truman and Tyler on Westminster Street, a serpentine bedstead from B.M. Cowperthwaite in the Bowery, assorted dishes and a gravy tureen from Richard Decker in Greenwich Street, and oak chairs, a table and a rocker from Brown & Bogert on Elm Street.

Receipts show that John was shipping a wide variety of items to northern markets. Fruits, probably grown on his farm, were sold to W.H. Blodget & Co. in Worcester, Massachusetts, a wholesale dealer in produce. He also dealt with Jeremiah Steelman, a grocer, ship chandler and lumber wholesaler in New York.

There were quite a few independent shippers on the peninsula in the nineteenth century. After all, people here grew up around the water. Most became familiar with boats at a young age and, as adults, were at home on the water. Shipping goods, like growing crops, was just another way to make a living. Today, it sounds romantic, heading off for the West Indies for a load of spices or delivering fresh seafood to the busy markets of New York. But in reality, it was simply business. Today's counterpart might be the owner of an eighteen-wheeler.

Bay Boats

Chesapeake Bay boats are the most graceful, colorful and romantic symbol of the maritime history of our peninsula. Most of the boats were designed for work—to dredge oysters, to fish crab pots or to haul cargo—but the best of them will also please the eye and make you smile when you see them move through the water. Boats are a bit like duck decoys—designed with function in mind, but when made by a true artisan, they surpass function and enter into a realm that could suggest art.

They come in a variety of designs, each made for an intended purpose. Perhaps the oldest is the Chesapeake log canoe, a design that goes back to the Native American presence in the bay. The boats are carved from logs hollowed out and joined together, and the length of the boat is determined by the dimensions of the logs available. Most are around thirty feet long and are propelled by sail.

The schooner, like my great-grandfather's *Panama*, is a workhorse of a boat, designed for carrying cargo. The schooner is a sleek, colonial-era design that typically has two masts, the one forward usually smaller than the one aft.

A Chesapeake Bay skipjack under sail, dredging for oysters on the Choptank River in Maryland.

The pungy holds a special place in my heart because there is evidence the name is derived from Pungoteague Creek in Virginia, on which we live. The design is similar to a schooner—sleek, two masts—but smaller.

The bugeye was very popular for dredging oysters in the 1880s and was similar in design to the log canoe and the pungy.

The most storied of the bay boats is the skipjack, whose presence on the bay was a symbol of Maryland's great oyster industry from the late 1800s to the mid-1900s. The skipjack fleet was once two thousand strong, but only a handful of the graceful old workboats remain. Skipjacks were designed as shallow-draft boats intended for dredging oysters under sail.

The modern symbol of the waterman's life is the Chesapeake Bay deadrise, so named for the shallow *V*-shaped angle of its hull. These handsome workboats with the forward cabin are very popular for fishing, crabbing and oystering. Modern deadrises are powered by diesel engines.

Buyboats were operated by seafood wholesalers who would convoy with oyster dredgers and purchase their catch while still on the water. These large

The modern watermen's boat is a Chesapeake Bay deadrise. This one is in the harbor at Tangier Island.

Crabs are sorted and packed in these waterfront shanties on Tangier Island.

boats typically have a rear wheelhouse and a spacious deck and cargo area. Buyboats are now being restored and used as recreational craft by owners who take advantage of the large decks and storage capacity.

The *Baltimore Sun*, in a July 27, 1906 article on the state of shipping in the Chesapeake Bay, said the sailing trade is dependent on this fleet of diverse craft, most of which are operated by independent owners rather than corporations. "On no navigable body of water in the United States is there a large trade so distinctive or so thoroughly local as the Chesapeake Bay trade of the sailing vessels. These vessels, none of them so very large, carry in great measure the bulk of the products of the state," reported the *Sun*.

The *Sun* estimated that some five hundred independent boats were working the bay, many of them conventional schooners found all along the coast, but also many vessels that were exclusively Chesapeake Bay designs. "Perhaps great fortunes are not made by the owners of bay craft, but you seldom find a schooner that does not pay something over her expenses. There are certain seasons for the different trades, and in between these times various charters can be got."

Wheat was in season when that article appeared in late July, and most of it was being shipped by smaller schooners, bugeyes, pungies and power barges. "Every day the smaller type of bay sailing vessels come in and discharge their cargoes," reported the *Sun*. "The wheat trade is profitable. The season begins about July 1 and ends about October 1. The first arrival of wheat this year came a few days earlier. The trade is steady during the summer, but there is a lapse of a month between the end of the wheat season and the corn trade. The corn business opens about November 1 and continues until December. A great deal of the grain brought to Baltimore for export comes from the counties of the Eastern Shore."

Lumber was also important to the port of Baltimore. "With only a few exceptions lumber trade is confined principally to the larger schooners. It is considerable on the bay, most of the lumber coming from the Virginia rivers or the tributaries on the Eastern and Western Shores of Maryland down near the Virginia line."

The *Sun* article said that in winter, most of the bay fleet is involved in oystering. "Some of them go in for dredging, but the larger ones prefer to become 'run boats' and 'buy boats,' buying stock from the oystermen and bringing it to Baltimore for re-sale. The trade of these sailing craft is almost as old as the commerce of Baltimore itself. There are vessels afloat today, and still in the trade, that were built back in the 1850s.

"The Eastern Shore, isolated as it is, must depend upon the water for its means of transportation, and the Western Shore, undeveloped in some parts, relies on the bay traders for its commercial intercourse," concluded the article.

The *Sun*'s reporter on bay boats, unfortunately unnamed, must have been a sailor himself. His detailed description of the different boats clearly shows an appreciation for nautical design. He wrote that the schooner is "conventional in all parts of the world and differs little from thousands of other schooners, but the real Chesapeake Bay characteristics are seen in the bugeye and pungy."

His description of the bugeye: "The bugeye is the one type that is expressive of the Chesapeake. Built of logs and sharp at bow and stern, there is a buoyancy to the hull that makes her an exceptionally fine sailor. Few bugeyes carry topmasts, but the fore and mainmasts are inclined at an angle that is almost violent. Leg-o'-mutton sails are used and before a wind of any volume the average bugeye can show a clean pair of heels to many steamers plying the bay. It is a type that originated years ago, and it is such a good one that there has been little change in the building of that style of craft."

On the pungy: "The pungy, too, is little different in appearance from the schooner, except that there is no waist. There is an absence of the graceful, sweeping curve from stem to stern, but when the pungy is under sail and heeling over with the lee rail awash and sails drawing well, there is gracefulness and beauty in plenty."

It's good to see a reporter who is enthusiastic about his work.

The Old Bay Line

While independent operators were a mainstay of commerce on the bay in the nineteenth century, it was the steam-powered sidewheeler that kept people and cargo on the move between Baltimore and Norfolk. If we use the analogy of sailing schooners being the eighteen-wheelers of the nineteenth century, the steamboats would have been huge double-decker Greyhound buses, with everything from farm products to manufactured goods stored below decks, and on the top deck would be scores of passengers traveling in comfort and enjoying the vista of the open bay.

If I could enter a time machine and travel back to any period I wanted, I'd pick the last quarter of the nineteenth century, when business and industry were flourishing in northern cities and the South had regained its sense of style and comfort. This was the era when the steamboat ruled the bay, when travel was not simply about the destination but rather the journey and the very pleasurable process of getting there. Today, we have cast aside the pleasures of the journey in favor of expediency, of making the journey as brief as possible. And so, we board crowded aircraft and sit elbow to elbow, our tray tables extended, a plastic cup of Coca-Cola and a packet of airline pretzels in our laps, and we furtively glance at our smartphones to see how many more minutes until we are herded off, put on conveyor belts and sent to concourse C to make our connecting flights.

Travel by steamship in the 1880s must have been the antithesis of this. Walter Lord wrote the foreword for Alexander Crosby Brown's 1961 book *Steam Packets on the Chesapeake*, a history of the Baltimore Steam Packet Company, better known as the Old Bay Line. In it, he said that steam travel combined the best virtues of North and South:

> *Where the Old Bay Line got its qualities remains a mystery. Perhaps through some magical blending of the best in the North and the South, made possible by the company's unique role in "bridging" the two regions. It is nice to think that the North has contributed its traditions of mechanical proficiency, making the ships so reliable; while the South has contributed its gracious ease, making the service so utterly delightful.*

Appletons' Journal of October 11, 1873, has an account by Robert Wilson of a trip from Baltimore aboard an Old Bay Line steamboat south to Old Point Comfort in Norfolk. On this fall trip, Wilson, with *lorgnette* in hand, described the bird life on the bay as the steamer left Baltimore, cleared the mouth of the Patapsco and headed south along the shores of Kent Island and past Love Point, across the mouth of the Chester River to Eastern Neck Island, which Wilson described as "no better shooting ground in the world for swans."

By fall, the ospreys that were so plentiful in the bay all summer had moved south. Wilson describes it this way: "The fishing-hawk has fled from the scenes of his domestic love and care, and betaken himself to Austral waters, not because he recks of the keen blasts of winter, but because he must follow his prey, and find his living where no ice-bound surface forbids his deadly plunge."

In other words, the osprey migrated south for the winter.

While the Old Bay Line steamships were the "stately pleasure domes afloat" on the greater Chesapeake, folks who lived along the rivers and creeks of the bay were probably more familiar with smaller, more maneuverable

This is the dining room of the NYP&N steamer *Elisha Lee. Nut Redden collection, Cape Charles Museum.*

craft that did not draw as much water. A. Hughlett Mason, a native of Harborton on Pungoteague Creek, wrote a book in 1973 titled *History of Steam Navigation to the Eastern Shore of Virginia*. Mason said that while the larger ships of the Old Bay Line were vital to commerce on the bay, the rural areas depended on smaller, shallow-draft vessels. "Even though everyone planned with enthusiasm a trip to Baltimore or Norfolk, the economy of the area was largely based on the excellence of transportation facilities for all kinds of commodities to and from Baltimore," Mason wrote.

Steam-propelled boats first appeared on the bay in 1813, and in 1838, steamboat service became available on Virginia's Eastern Shore when the *Virginia* stopped at what is now Harborton on its regular runs between Baltimore and Norfolk. This was a watershed event for transportation in the rural area. The railroad would not open for nearly a half century, so steamships provided local people a comfortable and comparatively rapid connection with the outside world.

"This section was inestimably more fortunate than the great land-locked areas of Virginia, which were forced to depend on stage coaches and wagons for transportation until the advent of the railroads," wrote Mason.

Steamboat service on the Eastern Shore was interrupted by the Civil War, but it resumed with a fresh start in 1867 when the Eastern Shore

Steamboat Company was organized. The company was founded by the Harlan and Hollingsworth boat-building firm of Wilmington, Delaware, which soon had a network of steamers operating from Baltimore to the Pocomoke River and down the bayside of the Eastern Shore to Northampton County.

The Eastern Shore bayside is characterized by numerous rivers or creeks running inland from the bay, creating narrow peninsulas of land locally known as "necks." Most creeks would have steamboat landings on both the north and south sides, thus serving clients from two necks. Pungoteague Creek, for example, had Hoffman's Wharf (now Harborton) and Boggs' Wharf on the southern shore and Evans' Wharf on the north side. Onancock Creek had the Onancock Wharf, where the Hopkins Brothers steamboat office was located, plus Finney's Wharf on the south side of the creek and Mears' Wharf (now Poplar Cove) on the north.

The purpose of the wharves and the steamboats, of course, was commerce. That's how the farmers got their strawberries and Irish potatoes to the northern market. And that's how their wives got material and fabric from Baltimore for making draperies and clothing. Local people made frequent shopping trips to the city, often spending a few days in a boardinghouse or hotel while shopping or attending to other business.

The steamer *Old Point Comfort*.

The steamer *Pocomoke* provided service from Baltimore to the Eastern Shore of Maryland and Virginia.

For children who grew up during the height of the steamboat era, it was a time they cherished throughout their lives. E. Spencer Wise grew up in Craddockville but spent a week each summer with his aunt and uncle at Finney's Wharf on the south shore of Onancock Creek. The wharf was built by three Finney brothers in 1871, two years after the Eastern Shore Steamboat Company began operating its shallow-draft sidewheel steamers between Baltimore and the Chesapeake Bay tributaries on the lower Eastern Shore.

Wise was born in 1914 and graduated from Virginia Tech with a degree in agriculture. In 1992, he wrote a memoir about his boyhood days at Finney's Wharf in the '20s. He wrote that the wharf was busy not only in the summer during his visits but year-round, shipping everything from farm crops to oysters. "Produce harvest began with strawberries in late April or early May," he said. "Later in May came spring peas and cabbage, followed by snap beans and onions in early June. Then in late June and early July Irish potatoes, the chief crop, were harvested. Late July was a slack time, but in August the sweet potato harvest began and continued until frost. Fall snap beans and lima beans were shipped in October, and then oysters would be shipped throughout the fall and winter months."

The steamboats exported local farm and seafood products, and they brought in stock for local mercantile stores as well as fertilizer from

The NYP&N not only ran the railroad, but it also competed with the steamboat companies.

Baltimore factories for local farmers. "There was a busy two-way traffic between Baltimore and the Eastern Shore wharfs," Wise wrote. "Merchants received their Christmas goods from the wholesale houses in Baltimore. Sweet potatoes that had been stored in kilns, live poultry, cedars to be used as Christmas trees, and holly were shipped to Baltimore. Barrels filled with goodies, including fresh pork from recent hog killings and dressed turkeys were shipped from the Shore to relatives and friends in Baltimore. Passengers traveled on the steamboats throughout the year."

The New York, Philadelphia and Norfolk Railroad

By 1884, the Pennsylvania Railroad had extended its track the length of the Delmarva Peninsula all the way to the Virginia Capes. The New York, Philadelphia and Norfolk Railroad (NYP&N), as the new line was called, was the dream of William L. Scott, a wealthy industrialist from Erie, Pennsylvania, who had the vision of linking the agricultural South with the industrial North by extending a rail line to the tip of the peninsula and from there across the Chesapeake Bay by barge.

In 1883, Scott bought three tracts of land from the Tazewell family for $55,000. The total acreage was more than 2,100 and included forest, farmland and waterfront between King's Creek and Old Plantation Creek on the western margin of the peninsula.

In 1884, he leased land to the railroad for a terminus and port, and he laid out 136 acres north of the port and designed the town of Cape Charles. Also that year, NYP&N bought its first sidewheel steamer and began extending rail service across the bay to Norfolk. The sidewheeler, appropriately named the *Cape Charles*, was unique in that it included not only a passenger lounge but also a deck laid with track sufficient to accommodate four railroad cars. Within a year, a marshy tract of remote bayfront had become a railroad hub, a link between the industrial North and the agricultural South.

Cape Charles City, as it was known then, resembled a gold rush frontier town, a Wild West movie set on the edge of a bay. The railroad had been easing its way down the peninsula for years, but when it made possible the bay crossing and the link with rail lines serving the South, it transformed forever the face of the countryside.

One of the early locomotives in the rail yard at Cape Charles.

The railroad ushered in an era of growth and prosperity unheard of on the Eastern Shore. Within a few years, towns were sprouting up where there had once been potato fields. In the past, commerce had centered on ports and shipping, but after 1884, farmers and businessmen turned their attention inland, toward the new railroad, which allowed quick access to markets in cities to the north and south. The coming of the railroad was truly a revolutionary event, one that would forever alter the history and culture of the Eastern Shore.

Several towns on the Eastern Shore were children of the railroad. Cape Charles is the most notable example, but Parksley, in Accomack County, was literally built by the railroad. In 1883, the site where the town now stands was farmland owned by Benjamin Parks, but within months, it would become an embryonic community of people, a town elaborately planned to the last street, park, church and schoolyard.

Benjamin Parks sold 160 acres to Henry R. Bennett and Samuel T. Jones of Dover, Delaware, and to Reverend J.A.B. Wilson of Philadelphia, who headed a development group called the Parksley Land and Improvement Company. Parksley was a planned community, with its core a business center laid out around the railroad station. A residential area surrounded this central core, and planners included five acres west of the railroad for a park and another one-acre parcel east of the railroad for a playground. Five acres were designated for a school, and two acres each were reserved for the two churches that applied for them.

Like Cape Charles City, Parksley quickly became a boomtown. Businesses sprung up around the railroad, and residential lots found willing buyers and investors. Although Parksley's founders were "northern capitalists," many Eastern Shore residents relocated there from nearby towns. Newspaper accounts of the day chronicled lot sales and business openings almost on a weekly basis. The developers of the community took an active part in the growth of the town. W.C. Wilson, secretary of the Parksley Land and Improvement Company, bought a parcel and planted it in fruit trees. The company president, S.T. Jones, shipped his herd of Jersey cattle to Parksley.

The railroad would eventually replace the steamboat when it came to transporting people and cargo, just as the steamboat had gradually supplanted the sailing fleet a century before. It didn't happen overnight, though. The steamboats had a loyal following, especially along the rivers and creeks that flowed into the bay. There had been a link between bayside farms and wharves and Baltimore merchants for generations,

Potatoes were loaded into barrels in the field and taken by wagon to the train station for shipment to market.

and this mutually beneficial relationship was strong. Steamships handled cargo and passengers from Nassawadox Creek north for years after the railroad was completed.

While the bayside had its link with Baltimore, the central portion of the peninsula, with the railroad running along its spine, had a tie to Philadelphia, New York and Boston. Trains ran from new towns such as Cape Charles, Keller, Onley, Tasley and Parksley north to Pocomoke City, and from there to Salisbury, Delmar, Seaford, Bridgeville, Harrington, Dover, Smyrna and finally Wilmington and Philadelphia.

The railroad and the steamships competed for years, but in the end, expediency won out. Like those of us who cast aside the pleasures of the journey for timely travel, it was thus when it came to railroad versus steamboat. A farmer could pick his strawberries in the morning, get them to auction that afternoon, and the railroad would have them in New York market stalls overnight, delivered in refrigerated cars.

The railroad developed a marketing system very similar to what the steamboats used a century earlier, when shipbuilders designed maneuverable, shallow-draft craft to navigate far upstream, reaching remote wharves to load potatoes and cabbages. The railroad built spurs to reach growers and seafood merchants far from the main lines. In 1876, a spur was built from Maryland to Franklin City, a community built on stilts overlooking Chincoteague Bay. Oystermen would transport their catch to Franklin City, and it soon would be on sale at the Fulton Market in New York. A spur to Kiptopeke opened in 1912, extending the rail five miles south of Cape Charles to the literal tip of the peninsula.

Getting what we grow to market is a constantly evolving process. It has involved water, rail, highways and air travel. And in all of these settings, it has been a part of our history and has transformed our community.

Chapter 3

THE RAILROAD AND THE PRODUCE EXCHANGES

A circular published in October 1929 by the United States Department of Agriculture revealed that over the previous decade (1920–29), the four contiguous counties on the southern tip of Delmarva produced more than 40 percent of all the potatoes shipped by rail in the entire United States. The counties were Accomack and Northampton in Virginia and Worcester and Somerset in Maryland. This rather startling statistic clearly demonstrates that the four southern counties were the leading producer of potatoes in the country.

How did that happen? Was it the soil, a favorable mix of bojac sandy loam? Was it the weather, the climate moderated and buffered by the bay on the western shore and the ocean on the east? Or were other factors coming into play?

According to the USDA circular, it was all of the above, along with improvements in transportation and the advent of some revolutionary and creative marketing efforts. Over the first three decades of the twentieth century, southern Delmarva led the nation in the production of both white potatoes and sweet potatoes. It was no coincidence that the peninsula was also one of the most prosperous rural areas of America during that period.

In 1884, the NYP&N Railroad opened, linking northern cities to the South via a railroad barge system spanning the Virginia Capes. The potential for local growers was obvious, but it took a few years to turn potential into profit. The USDA circular indicated that farmers may have been skilled at producing a crop, but most of them lacked marketing and sales experience.

Potatoes were sent to market in secondhand barrels intended for salt, flour and sugar and in used fertilizer sacks. "Farmers shipped potatoes to market in every sort and size of container," said the USDA report. "In fact, anything that could be induced to hold potatoes went into service."

Most potatoes were shipped in bulk, and few were graded according to size or quality. In some instances, farmers sent different varieties of potatoes in the same container. At the peak of harvest season, a mass of railroad cars would deliver potatoes to markets in Baltimore, Philadelphia, New York and Boston, causing the market to be flooded, resulting in lower prices for both dealers and farmers.

Eventually, farmers realized that they must work together for the common good and that consistency and quality would ensure brisk sales and premium prices. A group of Accomack and Northampton County farmers and businessmen joined together to create a joint-stock company that would sell the entire crop produced by members to the principal markets in the East. The organization would operate at cost and pay an annual dividend to shareholders.

The organization was incorporated on January 6, 1900, as the Eastern Shore of Virginia Produce Exchange, and it revolutionized the way produce was marketed on the Eastern Shore. "It was a remarkable success," said the USDA report. "The organization heroically attacked what were then the major marketing handicaps of the Eastern Shore, namely lack of a graded, standardized product and haphazard distribution among the markets. A standard barrel and a standard grade of potatoes were adopted."

The Exchange brought revolutionary new ideas to marketing farm produce, branding its potatoes under the copyrighted Red Star label and urging its growers to standardize on the Irish Cobbler variety. The Exchange put a small army of sales associates to work in all the major eastern markets, selling Red Star potatoes. Soon the Exchange was covering all of the United States east of the Rockies, Cuba and large sections of Canada during the potato season, which ran from June through August.

Farmers joined the Exchange by purchasing a share of stock for five dollars or by purchasing annual shipping privileges for one dollar, and they agreed to market exclusively through the organization during the harvest season. In exchange, farmers would receive an annual patronage dividend based on volume handled.

Volume rose steadily and extensively, and the two counties prospered. From 1900 to 1919, acreage in potatoes rose from eleven thousand to fifty-three thousand in the two Virginia counties and from two thousand

The Red Star label meant quality Irish, or white, potatoes.

to fourteen thousand in Maryland. And as acreage increased, quality and yield improved through the widespread use of commercial fertilizers, adding value at the marketplace.

The original Produce Exchange had stockholders only in Virginia, and with potato acreage on the rise in Maryland, there soon came a movement to have a similar marketing organization serving farmers in that state. The Peninsula Produce Exchange was founded in 1904 and was based generally on the model of the Virginia organization, except that it had no membership requirement and would accept shipments of any quantity from any farmer. The Maryland organization had a business volume of about one-fourth that of the Virginia Exchange, reflecting the acreage totals of the two states.

The Eastern Shore Produce Exchange in 1910 built a handsome, two-story brick office building in the town of Onley, which today still stands across the street from the town office. By 1915, the Exchange was doing $5 million in business, shipping on average a carload of potatoes for every hour of the year. A.J. McMath, a farmer and nurseryman who lived in Onley, was one of the organizers of the Exchange and became secretary/treasurer of the organization. He was interviewed by a magazine reporter in 1915 and explained how the Exchange revolutionized farm marketing:

> *"The system of marketing before the Exchange came was, in fact, just about as bad as it could well be," Mr. McMath told the reporter. "The*

These potatoes are waiting to be loaded into boxcars at the Onley station.

> *local buyers who took the farmers' produce found it to their interest to force prices as low as possible. Ten cents a barrel was the usual commission allowed them by the employing houses, and the lower the price at which they bought, the more barrels they could buy and the quicker they could turn over the money, and the better pleased were employing officers."*

Mr. McMath said the Exchange was successful because it did not sell on consignment, but instead confirmed the price with the buyer by wire before shipping. That way, the farmer knew exactly how much his crop would fetch him. Also, with 2,500 stockholders and 1,000 additional patrons, the Exchange controlled 75 percent of the market in the two counties. The Exchange guaranteed the quality of the product it shipped. Potatoes were inspected before shipment, and if they didn't meet certain criteria, they would either not be shipped or sold as a lower grade.

By 1913, the Exchange was shipping an average of 200 rail cars loaded with potatoes each day during the summer potato season. The record was 325 carlots a day, set in 1912. This small company in Onley was sending potatoes all over the country. The shipping book for July 15, 1913, recorded three carlots sold to South Bend, Indiana; six to Toronto; six to Providence; three to Boston; five to Detroit; twenty to Pittsburgh; three to Worcester; two

Produce was graded and labeled according to quality standards. These sweet potatoes were given the Bell label, assuring high quality.

The strawberry auction at Onley in May 1926 drew hundreds of farmers with wagons loaded with berries.

to Portland; five to Scranton; and one each to Allentown, Dayton, Hartford, Trenton, Newark, Rochester and Carbondale.

U.S. Census data show the dramatic increase in potato production over the first three decades of the Exchange. The total production of Irish potatoes on the Shore in 1899 amounted to 1,269,000 bushels; in 1909, 3,019,000 bushels; in 1919, 7,520,000 bushels; and in 1929, 10,198,000 bushels. The sweet potato production in both counties, according to the census, in 1899 was 2,525,000 bushels; in 1909, 3,143,000 bushels; in 1919, 4,179,000; and in 1929, 3,622,000 bushels.

The Exchange marketed far more than potatoes. It sold members' strawberries, cabbage, tomatoes and onions, although these crops were nowhere near the volume of Irish and sweet potatoes. The Exchange for many years operated strawberry auction blocks, where farmers would bring wagonloads of berries to be sold to the highest bidder. The largest auction block was in Onley, sandwiched between the brick Exchange office and the railroad track.

After World War II, farming changed on the Eastern Shore, as mechanization changed the world of agriculture just as the railroad had changed the world of shipping. Farms became larger and less labor dependent. Corn, soybeans and other grains became the important market crops. There still are a few reminders of the Farmers Exchange era. The once-impressive brick headquarters building is still there, currently in use as a church. And in local antique shops, you can now and then find a colorful "Red Star" label, once recognized nationwide as a symbol for quality.

Chapter 4

WHEN THE BERRY WAS BOSS

In the first half of the twentieth century, one of the most important crops for Delmarva farmers was the strawberry. Strawberries didn't cover massive fields like soybeans and corn do today, but farms were diverse in those days, and most farmers had a strawberry patch. Because the berries ripened and went to market in May, they constituted an early cash crop to revive a bank account that had lain dormant over winter.

There still are a few strawberry fields around, but in the late 1800s and early 1900s, Delmarva was known nationally for its strawberries, and it was a phenomenon that began somewhat abruptly. Two things happened to ignite the strawberry boom. The NYP&N Railroad made it possible to get fresh berries to New York markets overnight. Then, in 1900, the Eastern Shore of Virginia Produce Exchange was organized, providing growers on southern Delmarva with cooperative marketing and sales support, linking local producers with consumers in eastern cities and beyond.

The Exchange operated auction blocks adjacent to railroad stations, where farmers would bring their berries to be sold to the highest bidder. One of the largest auction blocks was at Onley, adjacent to the railroad track. At the peak of the season in 1938, sixty-five refrigerated railroad cars loaded with strawberries were shipped from Onley in a single day. During that season, nearly five million quarts of strawberries were shipped to market by the Exchange.

During the height of the spring season, NYP&N operated its Peninsula Strawberry Express, a daily stream of 150 rail cars heading north to Delmar,

Strawberries were picked in the field and taken to bowers to be packed in the shade to prevent spoilage.

The auctioneer at the Hallwood block drew the rapt attention of a child.

Wagons await the auction at Hallwood in 1926.

where the berries would be distributed around the country by NYP&N's parent company, Pennsylvania Railroad.

Strawberries were a labor-intensive crop that had to be picked, sorted and packed by hand. The berries were picked mainly by women and taken to strawberry bowers, temporary shelters in strawberry fields, where the berries could be handled in the shade. Quarts of strawberries would be packed into thirty-two-quart crates, which would be loaded onto trucks or horse carts for transport to the auction block. At the peak of the season, farmers would gather in railroad towns such as Onley, Exmore and Hallwood, lining the streets as they waited to get their crop to the auctioneer. As soon as the berries sold, they would be loaded onto rail cars and within hours would be in markets in New York and Boston.

Most of the berries were grown in small patches, but near Cape Charles, there was a strawberry field of more than one hundred acres. When the berries ripened in May and June, people who lived in Norfolk would take the ferry to Cape Charles to pick berries, living for a few days or weeks in temporary quarters.

But the importance of the strawberry market went beyond the fruit. Many local growers developed their own varieties of strawberry plants and sold them around the country. Brothers A.J. and George W. McMath of Onley were among the most successful plant propagators on the Shore. Growers would compete with one another to produce plants that had large fruits but still retained their sweetness and gentle texture. In May 1897, a Strawberry Exhibition was held at the Onancock Academy, and the McMaths took first place. Soon, the brothers began a successful nursery business in Onley, shipping strawberry plants to growers around the country.

Chapter 5

THE OYSTER FARM

I spent two winters in Alaska working as a photojournalist for the U.S. Air Force. Much of the work I did there was outside, and I can report that in winter, Alaska is a cold place. The coldest I've ever been, however, was on a day in November on the Choptank River with Captain Wade Murphy aboard the *Sigsbee*. Captain Wade was one of the handful of watermen still dredging oysters under sail, and a friend of mine who was related to Wade thought I might like to go along and document life aboard a working skipjack.

We were out on the water well before dawn on a very cold and breezy day when the sun didn't actually rise but became a luminescent cloud bank in the eastern sky. The Choptank was rolling and hissing, and when Wade's crew hoisted the sail the *Sigsbee* sat up like the old girl she was and got up on her hind legs. When the dredge went overboard, she paused and groaned and took a deep breath and caught her second wind.

Our day aboard the *Sigsbee* was memorable for two reasons. One, I had messed around on boats for most of my adult life, but I never had to make a living doing it. I'll always deeply respect the men and women who choose to work on the water. And two, Alaska can be cold, but there is no cold like being on the water when it's cold. It's a relentless cold that goes right through you, and I can still remember it.

The *Sigsbee* had been part of an earlier era of oystering on the bay. It was built on Deal Island in 1901 and had been one of more than one thousand shallow-draft centerboard boats made between the 1880s and 1910. Few classic Chesapeake Bay skipjacks survive today, and those that do are more

Top: Captain Wade Murphy aboard the *Sigsbee*.

Middle: Gordon Simmons of the *Sigsbee* crew lowers the sail as the ship returns to the harbor.

Bottom: The crew relaxes after a day on the water. *From left*: Gordon Simmons, Randy Wilson, Donnie Barrett, Tony Remeikis and Captain Wade Murphy.

likely to be known for participating in skipjack races than for dredging oysters. In fact, the *Sigsbee* sank during a race in 1991, was recovered and is now part of the Living Classrooms Foundation fleet.

The oyster industry fell on hard times beginning in the 1960s because of overfishing, destruction of habitat and the parasites MSX and Dermo. Annual catches in Virginia in the late 1950s surpassed four million bushels, but over the next three decades, those numbers plummeted. By the year 1996, the catch barely surpassed eighteen thousand bushels.

In the early 2000s, Virginia began a series of programs to rebuild public oyster reefs in the Chesapeake Bay and its tributaries, including the creation of oyster sanctuaries. Slowly, the population began to rebound. In 2013, the harvest was 400,000 bushels, and the following year it increased to 500,000.

Today, the oyster industry has reinvented itself, and the oysters you take home from the seafood shop will probably have a pedigree more associated with farming than sailing. Like hardshell clams, most commercial oysters are produced by aquaculture. Larval animals are raised indoors in a controlled setting, and then small adults, called spat, are planted in suspended beds in the natural environment until they grow to market size, which takes about two years.

Salt Marsh on the Half-Shell

My first experience with eating oysters happened when I was about nine years old. Someone gave my father a pint of seaside oysters, and my mother decided to make oyster stew. I didn't like oyster stew, so I asked her to give me some Campbell's creamy tomato. "Have you ever tried oyster stew?" she asked.

"No," I said. "I don't like it."

"You don't know what you're missing," said my father.

I knew exactly what I was missing. I saw that jar. It was full of huge, slimy, greeny-gray snot bugs.

"I like tomato soup," I replied.

My parents had their oyster stew, and I had tomato soup and a grilled cheese. They slurped and sucked and exclaimed how sweet and salty those oysters were. I finished my soup and took my plate and bowl into the kitchen and put them in the sink. My parents lingered over their coffee.

The pot with the oyster stew was still on the stove, and I took a look at it. The oysters were gone, but the broth left behind was spice-speckled cream tinted with golden butter. The serving spoon was still there, so I gave it a try. I had never tasted anything quite like it. The cream was rich and thick, and the butter added sweetness. I also tasted salt, but not the kind of salt you get with potato chips. The flavor was something I had experienced before but could not identify. There was sweet and there was salt, but the important element was the one I did not recognize.

And thus began my love affair with the oyster. Since then, I have had them in every conceivable way—single-fried, roasted, steamed, oyster fritters on a bun at the Chincoteague Volunteer Firemen's annual carnival. Oysters pair well with a wide variety of things: bacon, cheese, spinach and garlic. And you can combine them with other seafood to create a devilishly good casserole.

I've had bayside oysters and seaside oysters, oysters from Louisiana and oysters from New England. The only oysters I can honestly say I did not like were raw ones served in a small seafood restaurant in the town of Yachats, on the Oregon coast. The oysters were huge, big as a child's fist, and they were served unadorned in a little plastic cup of the sort they give you with pills in the hospital. I tried one but could not get past the tactile process of sucking that oyster out of the plastic cup. Oh, Momma, tomato soup, please. To be fair, the restaurant did not serve raw oysters on a regular basis, and it had clam chowder that was outstanding.

Like most things from the sea, the oyster is best when it is not fiddled with a lot. Open it and eat it. Put a small amount of cocktail sauce (ketchup and horseradish) on it to balance the salty flavor if you want, but otherwise leave it alone. It is difficult to appreciate raw oysters if you have not spent time in places where they grow. That means being out in the salt marsh in winter. I used to duck hunt a lot, and I still get out in the marsh with the camera. Sometimes I'll just go out there and walk around and take in the salt air.

Don's Seafood on Chincoteague Island has some of the best oysters I've ever had, and the reason is because Tommy Clark, the owner of the restaurant, also owns Tom's Cove Seafood, which grows oysters right there on the island. One day, a waitress at the restaurant asked if I enjoyed my dozen on the half-shell. "Yes, ma'am," I said. "They taste just like the salt marsh smells."

She gave me a look, not sure if that was a compliment or a complaint. People who don't spend time in salt marshes probably would not want to eat something that smells like one, and that puts them at a disadvantage when it comes to eating raw ones. If you are familiar with the salt marsh in winter, eating a raw oyster can take you there. You pick up the shell and gently slurp out the oyster. The first sensation is cold. The oyster has been on ice. The second sensation is salt—not potato chip salt but something wild and complex and natural.

The third sensation is difficult to explain. The flavor is the same as the salt marsh aroma. It has an organic quality, and it is derived from what the oyster has been eating. In winter, that means microscopic phytoplankton, the bits and pieces of spartina grasses that have been crushed by winter ice, attacked by bacteria, weathered into a rich soup of detritus. This plant decay is what you smell in the salt marsh in winter, the energy of last summer's sun being converted to food, photosynthesis in reverse. The oyster eats the detritus, and you eat the oyster. That's the element I sensed, but could not identify, the first time I tried oyster stew.

INDEX

D

E

F

G

H

R

S

T

U

W

ABOUT THE AUTHOR

Curtis J. Badger is a Delmarva native who majored in English at Salisbury University and, with the exception of four years traveling as a U.S. Air Force photojournalist, has enjoyed a career photographing and writing about his native coast. His books include *Salt Tide: Cycles and Currents of Life Along the Coast*; *Bellevue Farm: Exploring Virginia's Coastal Countryside*; *A Natural History of Quiet Waters*; *The Wild Coast*; *Exploring Delmarva*; *Wilderness Regained: The Story of the Virginia Barrier Islands*; and *Nathan Cobb's Island*, a children's book. He has won numerous awards for his writing and photography.

Lightning Source UK Ltd.
Milton Keynes UK
UKHW021933190822
407575UK00003B/121